Connections

YOUTHFUL
JERALD (JERRY) HARKNESS

ROLE MODEL
JACKIE ROBINSON

DETERMINATION
MOM - LUCILLE HARKNESS

MENTOR
COACH HOLCOMBE RUCKER

TOOK A CHANCE
COACH GEORGE IRELAND

ENCOURAGEMENT
COACH CHARLES SCHER

A Memoir
by
Jerry Harkness
Researched by Dan O'Brien

ISBN# 978-0-9987298-8-6

Printed in the U.S.A. by
Smith Printing, LLC, Ramsey, MN 55303
(800) 416-9099 • www.smithprinting.net

CONTENTS

ACKNOWLEDGMENTS

I would like to take this opportunity to thank those who encouraged me to write my memoirs, including:

Steve Watson, Director of Athletics, Loyola University of Chicago, who has been so supportive of the book, and Loyola athletes of the past and present.

Phillip D. Hale, Vice President for Government Affairs Office of the President, Loyola University of Chicago, who got White House approval for all things related to the book.

William Behrns, Loyola University of Chicago's Associate Athletics Director for Communications and Public Relations, who provided photographs and other Loyola athletic support.

Dr. Paul Smulson; DDS; whose persistent lobbying efforts resulted in the 1963 NCAA champion Loyola basketball team to be the first team inducted into the College Basketball Hall of Fame, provided photos and encouragement.

Donnie Walsh, the longtime Indiana Pacer executive, who bluntly stated, "You definitely should do it."

Former Indiana Pacer teammate Oliver Darden, my great friend, who wrote my foreword and constantly encouraged me.

My aunt, Clara Payne, who took on the challenge of researching our family's genealogy for years pretty much by herself, and finally got her due.

Dan O'Brien, journalist and sportswriter, who provided invaluable research and suggestions.

(continued)

Hallie Bryant, former Indiana High School "Mr. Basketball," Indiana University star, Harlem Globetrotter and the author of "Hallie's Comet: Breaking the Code," who offered merchandising and sales advice.

Dr. Greg Bell, the 1956 Olympic long jump gold medalist and author of multiple books, including an autobiography, "The Longest Leap," who gave me indispensable book advice.

Pete Cava, sports journalist and author of "Indiana Born Major League Baseball Players" and "Amazing Tales from the Chicago Cubs Dugout," who was extremely helpful throughout the process.

Mark Montieth, a free-lance writer for the Indiana Pacers, author of "Reborn" and "Passion Play", who provided support and Pacers photos.

Darlene Shamsid-Deen a dear friend who was generous with her time and administrative background.

And last, but hardly least, my lovely wife, Sarah, who encouraged me throughout the process and had to interpret and type my poor handwriting.

FOREWORD
by Oliver Darden

It was in the spring of 1963 that college basketball fans, including myself, became aware of Jerry Harkness and his Loyola University teammates because that was the year that Loyola won the NCAA basketball championship. However, Jerry will be remembered for more than just his basketball prowess. The more you know about Jerry's life, you will realize he is a remarkable person with significant achievements far beyond the world of athletics.

Although I was aware of his athletic prowess and his college basketball accomplishments in 1963, I didn't meet Jerry until 1967, when we became teammates on the original Indiana Pacers basketball team. After getting to know him, it became obvious this was a person of high moral character, intellect and extreme social skills. Although Jerry's professional basketball career was curtailed by a back injury, I would be remiss if I didn't state Jerry has been as successful off the court as he was on it.

Sports has long been a vehicle for African American athletes to give back and relate to the community, and Jerry has been a prominent example. Through his composure and grace, Jerry's accomplishments have had positive results throughout the Indianapolis community, the state of Indiana and the nation. After basketball, Jerry became known to a wider audience through his decade-long stint as a TV sports broadcaster and his involvement in numerous community and civic events. He has been a leader with the Indianapolis 100 Black Men organization, the Indiana Black Expo, the Indiana Human Rights Commission, the Police Athletic League and many other organizations.

Jerry is highly regarded by all who know him for his humility and temperament and is often said to be the right person at the right time for the right reason. He has been an invaluable contributor to growth in Indianapolis and Indiana, both socially and civically.

Jerry was born in New York and raised in Harlem, where he experienced the difficulty and complexity of city life. He honed his athletic skills with many of the top athletes of his era. Jerry's enrollment at Loyola University and the basketball success he achieved not only further shaped Jerry's character but forever changed the world of collegiate basketball.

Loyola remains the only Illinois college to win the NCAA tournament, but the most far-reaching impact of its championship was that it broke down barriers during an era of widespread segregation. During this time, particularly in the South, African Americans were barely recruited by many colleges, and those institutions that did offer scholarships were selective. Unwritten rules limited the opportunities for African American players. Loyola was one of the first universities to start four African Americans. That was revolutionary in an era when some schools started none, and virtually no schools started more than two.

Loyola's accomplishment definitively demonstrated to other schools that the recruitment of African American athletes was neither detrimental to their mission nor was it viewed negatively by school alumni or the general public. Its athletes were unique in their skills, dedicated to their goal and disciplined enough to overcome the challenges facing them. Needless to say, Jerry was the captain of this team. His leadership, maturity and quiet confidence helped provide the fortitude necessary to face hostile crowds with aplomb.

The final vestige of the southern attitude toward integration was eliminated during the 1963 tournament. Mississippi State University and state government officials had a policy of not allowing their teams to compete against opponents with African American players. The MSU board of regents, however, voted to play the game and the team surreptitiously left town in the dark of night to play against Loyola in the Mid-East Regional in East Lansing, Mich.

Jerry and his Loyola teammates merely had a goal of having a successful basketball season but wound up making history in ways they could not have foreseen. Their success and example inspired a multitude of African Americans, athletes and otherwise that established a new template – one that enabled me to become the first African American to be elected captain of the University of Michigan basketball team in 1966.

We all thank you, Mr. Harkness.

Oliver Darden

INTRODUCTION

As I tossed around ideas in my head as to what I should use as a title for my memoirs, one word, one theme, kept coming back to me: Connections. I think all of our lives are determined to a large extent by the human connections we make and I can't think of anyone for whom that holds true more than yours truly. Relatives, coaches, teachers, mentors, friends and role models I have never met all have played a part in what I've accomplished and who I've become. A number of them were there early on trying to lead me toward the right path, others entered my life at later stages and some have re-entered my life at various times.

My first and most natural connection was my mother. I watched Mom overcome incredible odds and adversity to raise my sister and me. But despite all of my wonderful earthly connections I firmly believe there had to be something more powerful, spiritual if you will, that kept me going and guided me in the right direction toward my goals.

Here's my story!

Chapter 1
SPRINGFIELD TO THE WHITEHOUSE

I looked up in the State House Rotunda in Springfield, Illinois, not fully realizing I was a step closer to a dream I never, ever, thought would come true. Rich Rochelle, Jack Egan and I – college basketball teammates at Loyola University of Chicago – were invited to speak on the floor of the State Senate to commemorate the 50th anniversary of Loyola's NCAA basketball championship in what is now called "Division I."

I was filled with a tremendous sense of pride but also a sense of wonder, almost disbelief. Sure, the rational side of me knew how I got there. But I had to figuratively pinch myself, wondering how this poor kid from Harlem could end up addressing these Illinois lawmakers.

When it came time for me to speak, I related a few fond basketball memories. To say playing on that championship team changed my life would be a massive understatement. In addition, that team – with four African Americans in the starting lineup – helped change attitudes. I stressed the importance of sports and how the games can provide much more than athletic competition.

I also told of a memory that is not so sweet.

In 1967 – only four years after I captained Loyola to the national title – my family and I were denied a vacant apartment on Winona Street in Chicago because of our race. I have since received a full apology from the person who turned us away. To my surprise – and relief – I received a loud ovation from the lawmakers.

After signing autographs and taking photos with the dignitaries, Rich, Jack and I received a tour of the Illinois Capitol. Our first stop – for cake and conversation – was at the office of the President of the Illinois Senate, John Cullerton, a Loyola-Chicago graduate. From there we proceeded to the office of Michael Madigan, Speaker of the Illinois House of Representatives, another Loyola alumnus.

1

Meeting Barack Obama in 2008 Campaign. (I'm in the cap)
Courtesy Photographer Michael Patton, Sr.

Egan, a longtime Chicago-area attorney who is attuned to Illinois politics, whispered in my ear that Speaker Madigan had played a major role in Barack Obama's rise in Illinois politics. That set me to thinking of the proverbial impossible dream: Could we be invited to the White House to meet the President of the United States? I had met Barack Obama in 2008 in Indianapolis during one of his first Presidential campaigns. But a visit to the White House? That would take it to a whole new level. And what could be more appropriate than the 50th anniversary of a predominantly black championship team from Chicago meeting our nation's first President of color, a former Illinois politician and Chicago resident?

Egan was already on top of it. He had talked to Speaker Madigan about that very possibility. Loyola's Vice President for Government Affairs, Philip D. Hale – the school's political liaison in Springfield – was also busy pushing for the White House invitation.

After I returned to my home in Indianapolis, I met with U.S. Congressman Andre Carson to see if he could help the 1963 Loyola Ramblers obtain an invitation to the White House. Congressman Carson put a staff person right on it. I provided some background information on our championship season, including a DVD of "The Game of Change," a documentary produced by my son, Jerald, which focuses on Loyola's landmark game against an all-white Mississippi State team during the 1963 NCAA tournament.

A few weeks later I received a call from Phil Hale that sent me into orbit. Phil told me the White House needed the names, addresses and Social Security numbers of the players from the championship team. Even over the phone, Phil could sense my mind was practically spinning out of control.

"Calm down, Jerry," Phil said. "This is not a confirmation of a White House invitation."

In terms of action on the Presidential level, things were moving pretty quickly. Yeah, I realize that now. At the time, it seemed like an eternity.

Two weeks later Phil called again with the three most beautiful words I've ever heard: "We are in."

I was too excited to hold back. I called Les Hunter, another Loyola teammate. I then called Egan and the rest of my six surviving teammates at that time. I wanted to be the first one to tell them ... before they were contacted by Loyola officials. We all wanted to shout, broadcast or – for those more technically current than I am – post on social media the news of our White House invitation. However, we received explicit instructions not to tell anyone outside of our wives and closest relatives. Finally, after another perceived eternity, our travel arrangements arrived.

And so, on July 10, 2013, seven players from Loyola's championship team, their wives and a small contingent of school officials arrived in Washington. We went to our hotel rooms, quickly freshened up and then back to the lobby where we all gathered for a trip to Capitol Hill. We met U.S. Senator Richard Durbin of Illinois in his office and presented him with a signed basketball. While socializing there, Minority House Speaker Nancy Pelosi and Illinois Congresswomen Jan Schakowsky, among others, stopped by.

Ron Miller on the left, myself and Jack Egan enjoyed talking with
Illinois Senator Richard Durbin in his office.
Photo courtesy the office of U.S. Senator Dick Durbin.

Upon returning to the hotel, Phil Hale instructed us to be in the lobby by 10 o'clock the next morning for a trip to the White House. None of us was a second late. We boarded the mini-bus for the White House. Unfortunately, due to some scheduling challenges, our wives couldn't join us on this one. But they gave us a warm send-off from the hotel, waving and cheering as they wished us a memorable meeting with President Obama.

A series of security and procedure checks ensued, but at this point I didn't mind. We were "in" – not yet inside the Oval Office, but "in." We were dropped off at a guard house at the White House gate where three police officers checked our credentials. Phil Hale provided additional written information. After a wait of about 20 minutes, we embarked on a short walk to the White House. During our walk, I asked teammate Ron Miller, "Isn't that John McCain filling somebody's ear on the other side of the street?" (I always ask Ron such things since he follows politics like I follow the Indiana Pacers). Ron confirmed it was, indeed, Senator McCain.

We were escorted to the West Wing of the White House and then to the Roosevelt Room where two armed guards awaited. Valerie Jarrett, Senior Adviser to the President and Assistant to the President for Public Engagement and Intergovernmental Affairs, was there to greet us. Ms. Jarrett lived up to her "Public Engagement" role as she made it her business to speak with everyone in our group.

I hope I was equally engaging during our conversation but, even in the White House some things are unavoidable. I had to ask for directions to the restroom. I could sense someone following me, and as I closed the door to this very small room I knew immediately someone had come to a halt right outside the door. I was prepared for a possible encounter upon my exit and I wasn't disappointed as a tall, heavyset, uniformed guard evaluated and inspected me before making eye contact. It was a bit unsettling at first, but I realized he was only doing his job. And yes, he did it well.

I rejoined the others in the Roosevelt Room. Time seemed to freeze again. As the minutes ticked away, it seemed as if hours had gone by. As I later told a reporter, I was so nervous I was "tingling in my fingers and toes." Finally, the President of the United States, Barack Obama, opened the door to the Oval Office and with a simple, "Hi, ya," invited us in.

He introduced himself individually to every member of our party as a photo unknowingly was taken with each player. I introduced myself as "Jerry

The Loyola group met President Barack Obama in the oval office White House on July 11th, 2013. From left to right, Loyola's Vice President for Government Affairs, Phillip D. Hale, Head Basketball Coach Porter Mosher, Guard Jack Egan, Guard Dan Connaughton, In front is former Asst. Vice President Athletic Director Dr. M. Grace Calhoun, Center Les Hunter, President Barack Obama, Judy Ireland, Forward Captain Jerry Harkness, Guard Ron Miller, Forward Chuck Wood, Center Rich Rochelle, Loyola University's Former President Father Michael Garanzini and Former Vice President of Athletics Tom Kelly. *Courtesy White House Photo by Pete Souza.*

Harkness, Captain of the Loyola Ramblers." He shook my hand with that warm, genuine smile and put me at ease when he called me, "Cap."

When it came time for the President to address the 1963 Ramblers, he first asked for "The Captain" to come forward. Smiling, he said, "What ya got?"

I presented the President with a double-pictured plaque. The top picture was a team photo. The bottom picture was a history-making handshake between Mississippi State captain Joe Dan Gold and me prior to our win over the Bulldogs in the Regional of the 1963 NCAA tournament. It marked the first time a team from the Deep South played in the Division I NCAA tourney against black ballplayers.

I had so much I wanted to tell the President, such as about the previous time I had met him in Indianapolis and other racial experiences we had in the South. I also wanted to compliment Mississippi State's team for sneaking out of Mississippi to play us. Then I remembered Les and Jack had to make presentations. I didn't want to dominate everyone else's time, so I stopped

I made plaque presentation to President Barack Obama as Dan Connaughton, Les Hunter, and Ron Miller look on. *Courtesy White House Photo by Pete Souza.*

talking. Valerie Jarrett jumped in and introduced Judy Van Dyck, daughter of our late coach, George Ireland. Judy told how her father loved us as his own sons and protected us. Like most athletes, we always find comments like that from coaches amusing.

As we stood around talking basketball with President Obama, who had played high school basketball and remained a fan of the game, Ron Miller brought up something that was in all the scouting reports on Loyola when we played: Jerry rarely goes to his right. Ron asked the President, "Being left-handed like Jerry, can you go to your right?" The President had us all laughing when he said 'No, I cannot go right too well, but I am so fast they still cannot keep up with me.'

I did not think of it at the time, but Egan later pointed out the political context of going left but not right, and we chuckled. I think all of us would have agreed that President Obama, the leader of the free world, was just one of the guys when it came to talking basketball.

On another subject, the President shared with us that he has to do what he believes is right, whether it is popular or not. His approval rating was in the high 50s at the time but I doubt he wavered from that course even when his ratings weren't as high.

Les Hunter presents Loyola jersey to President Obama as the players join in.
Courtesy White House Photo by Pete Souza

Before leaving the Oval Office, I told the President I enjoyed volunteering for him during his last campaign, for which he was grateful. As I continued to walk, I kept thinking, *Jerry, couldn't you have thought of something better than that to say?*

I had no real regrets, though. The White House visit was one of the best experiences of my life, especially with my Civil Rights background. I had received a second meeting with the first black President of the United States, this time with an audience at the White House. Aside from the birth of my children and meeting my wife, Sarah, being recognized by President Obama was the greatest thrill of my life.

As we got on the bus to go back to the hotel, I thought about how fortunate I have been in meeting people such as Dr. Martin Luther King Jr., General Colin Powell, Jesse Jackson, candidate Barack Obama and finally, President Barack Obama. Wow!

It was another one of those pinch-yourself moments when I had to ask myself, "Could this be true?"

I then thought of something I've tried to instill in others: Try your best and never give up. You'll be surprised at what you can accomplish.

I came away smiling broadly, realizing once again that it was true.

Chapter 2
TOGETHERNESS IN HARLEM

May 7, 1940 – Franklin Delano Roosevelt won the California Democratic primary en route to his third term as President of the United States; British Prime Minister Neville Chamberlain appointed Winston Churchill to lead Britain's war effort against Germany; playwright William Saroyan refused the Pulitzer Prize for his Broadway hit, "The Time of Your Life;" and the St. Louis Cardinals thumped the Brooklyn Dodgers, 18-2. Of course, the world took no note of an event I consider fairly important: the birth of Jerald Harkness at Harlem Hospital. I grew up a few blocks away at 2760 8th Avenue, between 146th and 147th Street.

I was always proud of my roots because people all over the world are so intrigued with Harlem. They want to know all about it. Was it clean? Dirty? Was it gang-infested? Did you ever go to the Apollo Theater? Was it crowded? Was it an exciting place to live?

Yes, it was exciting – and different – to have so many black folks with so much in common, all in such close proximity. For example, I can remember the entire neighborhood celebrating a Joe Louis knockout victory, with people opening their windows and cheering in unison, making a loud, beautiful echo in the streets. As a six-year-old, I saw Harlem turn out in full force – an estimated 200,000 people – for a parade honoring Louis. Although he was from Detroit, he spent a day on a Harlem sidewalk buying and giving away food.

Because of segregation you would always run into African American celebrities on Harlem's streets, and I'm convinced I ran into a lot of future African American celebrities as well. I remember seeing the great musician Duke Ellington, boxing champion Sugar Ray Robinson, baseball star Willie Mays and the writer James Baldwin, who had attended my high school, De-Witt Clinton. I also saw actresses Leslie Uggams and Cicely Tyson and tap dancer Bill Robinson, who lived in the upscale Dunbar Apartment where my grandparents resided. I even heard an African American Muslim minister named Malcolm X speak on the Harlem sidewalks. Harlem overflowed with black culture ... and I loved it.

When I graduated from P.S. 139 Junior High we had our prom at the Savoy Ballroom on Lennox Avenue, between 140th and 141st streets. At the Savoy, billed as "The World's Finest Ballroom," I also listened to the great bands of Duke Ellington, Louis Jordan, Dizzy Gillespie and Chick Webb. I wondered why so many white men sat up front, listening closely to the featured bands. I found out later they were copying the styles of the black musicians.

In addition to the local celebrities, Harlem was a mecca for black entertainers from other cities. They not only came to perform but also simply to visit. Almost all the businesses in Harlem – the candy stores, drug stores, dry cleaners, florists, grocery and clothing stores – were owned by African Americans. I truly enjoyed growing up there and was never bored. I played marbles, tag, stickball and hide-and-seek in the streets.

Attending Abyssinian Baptist Church was another highlight. My family got all dressed up to listen to Reverend Adam Clayton Powell (I wondered why he was so light-skinned). My family also attended Union Baptist Church at 145th and 8th Avenue.

We used to leave elementary school every Thursday afternoon at one o'clock to go to Union Baptist for religious education. That started my Bible study foundation. I truly believe the elimination of similar programs around the country is one reason we are having so much trouble with our children today. I volunteered with the Indianapolis 100 Black Men mentoring program in public schools for more than 30 years. Mentors aren't even allowed to talk about religion unless the children bring it up. I know it really helped my upbringing. I am sure it would be beneficial to some of our youth of today.

Chapter 3
OUR GENEALOGY

Let's see, where should I start? Aunt Clara is probably a good beginning.

At age 12, my aunt, Clara Bailey Payne, became bored while visiting our family's summer home in Orange, Virginia, about 30 miles northeast of Charlottesville. As a result, she started exploring the attic and closets around the house. She collected – and hid – all kinds of items, including letters and documents. This, of course, was long before television commercials and internet ads promoting the tracing of ancestry through DNA. Little did she know, it was the beginning of one of the best family trees I have ever seen. Aunt Clara has accumulated thousands of items for documentation, including family pictures, birth certificates, death certificates and marriage licenses. She has made numerous trips to the Orange County Courthouse and library, and interviewed many family members, friends and others in the Orange, Virginia, area.

Aunt Clara has donated a number of her discoveries to the Smithsonian Institute and to the new National Museum of African American History and Culture in Washington, D.C.

Frank Ellis Estate in Orange, Virginia, the fifteen-acre family home was a good change of scenery in the summer from the crowded streets of Harlem to open space in the south.

At the time of this writing, she has researched eight generations, going back to 1790 with slaves Aaron and Hannah May. They were the parents of one of my favorite ancestors, Squire May, who was born in 1824, somewhere around Orange, Virginia. Squire, who was noted as a chair maker, spent 41 years enslaved. He married Clara (Clia) Madison May, a slave on the Montpelier plantation that was the home of James Madison, the fourth President of the United State. Squire and Clara became free about four years before her passing in 1869. Later, at some point in the 1880's, Squire married Rose Madison May.

Montpelier Plantation home of the 4th President of the United States, James Madison. The 2,700-acre Madison homestead is operated by the Montpelier Foundation and the Orange County African American Historical Society. Many of my ancestors are traced back to Montpelier, over three-hundred slaves are documented from the Madison era.

Squire was a faithful member of Pamunkey Baptist Church in Orange, Virginia, for 67 years as both a slave and a free man. During that time, self-taught, he started giving sermons in his home. His Christmas sermon, delivered on his 77th birthday (December 15, 1901), was published in the 1901 Christmas day edition of the Lexington (Virginia) Gazette.

Here are some excerpts from that sermon:

"... for without honor you cannot please God. So many these days are drinking whiskey and killing time and say they are going to Heaven. They have so little honor, not enough to tell their brother how-to-do. But the Master says you cannot reach that kingdom because your arms will be too short. I call no names but hundreds are guilty of the stain. Now, as Paul says, 'I was a child. I had childish ways, now it becomes me to lay down childish ways and to think like a man, speak like a man and act like a man.' So, let all God's children come together on Christmas day and rejoice like strong men in the service of God. Then we can eat and drink that which is good."

Pamunkey Baptist Church opened its doors in 1774 and rebuilt in 1854. One of my favorite ancestors Squire May attended the church for sixty-seven years as both a slave and a free man.

Squire May died at the age of 85. The funeral at his residence was conducted by Reverend W.J. Decker, pastor of North Pamunkey Baptist Church. He was eulogized before a large crowd of both colored and white friends as a man of the highest integrity as well as a God-fearing, Christian man. Six well-known prominent white gentlemen acted as pallbearers.

The Lexington Gazette published many of his lessons, entitled "Squire May's Sermon." A picture of Squire May and his second wife, Rose Madison, can be found in the National Museum of African American History and Culture in Washington, D.C.

Clara (Clia) Madison had two daughters at a very young age by a white enslaver. Squire and Clara (Clia) had seven children, including Polly May, who married Frank Ellis Sr. Their union produced 13 children, including my grandmother, Eliza Ellis Bailey (who spoiled me rotten). Eliza married my grandfather, Moses Bailey. Three children came from this union: my aunt

Squire May and second wife, Rose Madison May.

Clara, my uncle Fred Bailey and my mother, Lucille Bailey Harkness. My mom married my father, Lindsay "Sonny" Harkness. Their children were Ronnette, who passed in infancy, my sister Marlene, and me.

Family photo. Key members - bottom left, my sister Marlene, Aunt Clara, and me on the end; Middle row on the right, my mom Lucille; 3rd from the right, Grandmother Eliza Bailey; on the left end, Aunt Jean; top row left, mom's friend Al, then Uncles Fred Bailey, Wiley Salmonds, and Arthur Payne; 3rd from right, Grandfather Moses Bailey.

Antique items were donated to the National Museum of African American History by Aunt Clara Bailey Payne

A representative from the Montpelier Foundation, which operates James Madison's 2,700-acre plantation, visited with Aunt Clara in Harlem for two days to examine all of the documents, letters and other items she has collected on Montpelier. The foundation has used some of Clara's research for its major permanent exhibition on slavery.

My uncle, Fred Bailey, drove us from Harlem to our family home in Orange, Virginia, during the summertime. We made sandwiches for the trip and had a cooler of Kool-Aid and water. My uncle never wanted to stop along the way, but one time we had to because I needed to use the restroom. That was my first segregation experience. I was directed to a dingy bathroom at a gas station that had a "For Colored Only" sign above the entrance. When I came out I saw an entrance with the words "Whites Only" over it. When I got back to the car I asked my uncle and mom what that was all about. He did not answer because he was mad at me for having to go to the bathroom; he said I should have gone in Washington, DC. For him, it was yet another example of having to deal with being looked upon as second-class citizens.

When we arrived at our home of 15 acres, the world seemed to come alive - chickens and rabbits running all over the place, horses standing in the barn, cows mooing and pigs eating anything you threw to them in their pen. The water in the well, which you lifted with a bucket and drank from a dipper, was cold and tasted so much better than city water. The foods from the garden and cornfield were fresh, and grapevines climbed all around the front porch where we sat together. Large trees shaded the porch but were out of the way of the cornfields that reached all the way out to our property-line fence. A small spring ran through the property, and you could drink from it. I used to race my uncle from the porch to the road alongside the cornfield, but never won despite getting a head start. I could never understand that because I was the second-best sprinter among all my friends in Harlem. I didn't care if my uncle was in his twenties and I was ten.

My first morning there, I was awakened by a rooster. I looked out the window from bed and saw my great-uncle Fred Ellis working with two horses in the cornfield. I looked at the clock and saw it was 5:30 a.m. I thought to myself, I hope he doesn't call me to help.

That afternoon we went into town to watch some of the locals play baseball; this time I saw the same signs for "colored" and for "white" above two water fountains. While the game was going on, a truck filled with white teenagers shouting racial slurs drove by, and many of the black players yelled back at them – another experience that confused me.

Family and friends gather in Virginia to celebrate Aunt Clara's Genealogy recognition. Front row, L-R - Clara, Kiley, Zann, and Marie; Second row, L-R - Sarah, Jerald, Barbara, Kara and myself.

I also had the unpleasant experience of using an outhouse. And I watched a family member chase down a chicken, ring its neck and pluck the feathers so we could eat it for dinner that night. The ham and other poultry coming from the meat house was a little salty, but I was happy because we had all we could eat.

We also visited President Thomas Jefferson plantation, called Monticello, in Virginia near Charlottesville. I was amazed at the huge clock above the entrance inside the house and was intrigued with the beds built into the walls to help get away from the cold, and how they used to sleep sitting up. It was also interesting to see where the slaves stayed and worked. I visited Monticello again a few years later after reading up on Jefferson and asked the curator if Jefferson had fathered any children with his slaves. She abruptly said, "No" and scolded me for having the nerve to ask such a question. I just smiled and moved on.

I truly enjoyed my summer trips to Orange, Virginia - so peaceful, so much open space, so clean and refreshing. The dirt on the ground even looked clean, with a dark rust-color. It was a good change of pace, but it was always the right time to go back to Harlem.

Chapter 4
EXPERIENCES IN HARLEM

I only vaguely remember my father leaving for World War II. I was barely three when he enlisted. He was eventually stationed in Manila. I have a better memory of my dad coming home from the war, late at night. I yelled, "Daddy!" and my sister and I jumped into his arms and told him how happy we were to see him. My Mom was happy to see him, too. I still play that scene in my mind from time to time.

I don't know what happened after that. My dad got a construction job and was paid weekly, but for some reason there were weeks he didn't come home with a paycheck. My Mom would have a fit and shout at him. My dad wasn't a drinker or gambler, but the company he worked for struggled to make ends meet and didn't always pay on time. That brought sadness and stress into the house, and before I knew it he was gone.

While in elementary school, I was always having to try to hide the fact I had holes in my shoes by putting cardboard in the soles. It really became a problem when it rained and the cardboard got soggy. I would have to try to push it back in or pull it completely out before a classmate could detect it. If caught, I blamed it on the school for not cleaning the floors.

"Look at that cardboard paper on the floor, sticking to my shoes! Why don't the janitors clean up around here?"

I also blamed Mom for not being able to buy me new shoes when I needed them. Later, I realized we were among thousands of other struggling New York City families, just trying to survive. I began to understand the pressure that was on my mom, and I resented Dad for leaving us that way.

It got so bad that Mom had a nervous breakdown and was admitted into Bellevue Hospital. My Aunt Clara took us in and my grandparents also helped considerably. I don't remember going to visit Mom, but I'm sure Aunt Clara and my grandparents did. Mom stayed in the hospital for about two months. Aunt Clara told my sister and me that my mom needed a lot of rest.

That meant no noise. We tried to take care of her the best we could. I don't think I'm alone when I say it hurts now when I think of all the pressure I put on my mom, not realizing what she was going through.

I'll never forget my mom. After resting up from her hospital stay, she told us we were going to work together to make things better. It took a month or two but she finally achieved her first goal: she got a job in a hospital, which helped restore her confidence. I'll never forget the glow on her face, one I hadn't seen in quite a while. When you realize she had very little education, suffered a nervous breakdown, had to raise two children without my dad and still fought all the way back to support her children, you can understand why I'm overwhelmed by her accomplishments. She was a great mother and was always there for Marlene and me ... always! All that I've accomplished started with my mother, and she is the main reason I am writing this book. We were never a family that said, "I love you," or showed affection or had long talks, but we knew she loved us very much.

In prayer, just riding alone in the car, I often thank God that I had a mom who never gave up. She was determined to make it. As I look back, there were more good times than bad times in Harlem. We always had a wonderful Christmas, with toys and clothes I got from family members. After a while, I began to realize I wasn't as bad off as a lot of children in my school.

I should make the distinction that we lived in Uptown Harlem. There wasn't much crime there, nor were drugs prevalent. It was really a good, positive environment. We were fairly close to the Sugar Hill area, which was roughly bounded by West 155th Street to the north, West 145th Street to the south, Edgecombe Avenue to the east, and Amsterdam Avenue to the west. A number of prominent African Americans grew up and lived in the Sugar Hill area, among them W.E.B. Du Bois, Thurgood Marshall, Adam Clayton Powell Jr., Duke Ellington and Cab Calloway. The actress and singer Leslie Uggams, who was appearing on national television shows by age ten, also was from that area. She hosted her own variety show on television in 1969, becoming the second African American to do so after Nate King Cole in the Fifties. Her show included weekly sketches dealing with the lives of middle-class blacks in a large American city, entitled "Sugar Hill."

My grandparents lived at the Dunbar Apartments, between 149th and 150th streets and bordered by Frederick Douglass Boulevard/Macomb Place, and Adam Clayton Powell Jr. Boulevard. The Dunbar, named for African

My sister Marlene and I inside the Dunbar Apartments in Harlem.

American poet Paul Laurence Dunbar, had its own policeman assigned to security. Non-residents needed permission to enter. In addition to my grandparents, Dunbar residents included the dancer Bill "Bojangles" Robinson, explorer Matthew Henson, A. Phillip Randolph, Paul Robeson and W.E.B. Dubois.

In that environment, I learned early on that some of the greatest pleasures are the simple ones. I enjoyed throwing snowballs from the piles in front of our building or firing a cap pistol that would "pop" when you pulled the trigger. I enjoyed Halloween when we dressed up in old clothing and pretended to be pirates or bums. We didn't have to wait for the first snow to have our first "snowball" assaults. We would put flour in a long nylon stocking and swing it at friends or guys from another block. The flour would blow out onto your target's clothes (no faces), leaving a big white spot. It was great fun until guys started putting rocks in the flour. Yeah, some guys had to take things to a less desirable level.

BB guns or air rifles could be the source of great fun or a major annoyance, like when guys shot at me when I was learning to play basketball or dodgeball. I think every kid on the block owned, or at least wanted, a BB gun, especially the Red Ryder air rifle (the one featured in the 1983 film, ("A Christmas Story"). It was designed to look like a genuine Old West rifle and borrowed its name from the popular Red Ryder comic strips. We were fortunate no one got badly hurt from the BBs. As in the movie, there was always the threat that some kid would "shoot his eye out." To the best of my knowledge, that never happened. But, boy, did those tiny pellets sting!

I mostly enjoyed the games in which I could use my speed, such as stickball. Most of the time I was the last one caught when we played tag. We ran races in the street, and I always finished second behind my best buddy, Frank Dowell.

While I had a lot of wonderful times in Harlem, there were also some negative experiences, such as a situation that occurred when I was ten or eleven years old. A bully from the neighborhood put a knife in my back and directed me to the front door of an apartment building. He told me to go into the building and walk up the stairs, or he would stab me in the back. I asked him what he wanted. He told me to keep walking.

I kept thinking about the money I earned from selling *The Amsterdam News* outside the subway train station at 145th Street. I had just bought some candy and was going to use the balance of my cash to go to the movie theater the next day. Finally, we got to the roof. He told me to open the door and go in. I was scared and nervous, until I remembered people go on the roof in Harlem all the time. But this time no one was there. He told me to empty my pockets. I hesitated and he stabbed at me a couple of times and said "You heard me, I'm going to cut you the next time!" Then I heard somebody yelling from the rooftop across the street, "Hey, stop!" At that moment I ran for the door, opened it and felt a thump. He had thrown the knife and hit me in the back, but with the handle rather than the blade. I ran down the stairs. He yelled, "Stop!" I kept running until I reached home. When I told my mother, she asked, "Who is he? Who is his mother?" I said "That's all right mom, he didn't hurt me." The next day, I ran into the bully and he threatened to hurt me really badly if I told anybody about the knife.

I couldn't get the incident off my mind, so I went to the candy store to speak with the owner, Mr. Pew, who I talked to often. I didn't tell him about the knife. I just told him about this guy that kept bothering me, and I didn't know what to do. Mr. Pew said, "You will have to fight him." I said, "But he's so much bigger than I am." Mr. Pew said, "I know who he is and you are right, he is older and bigger, but you will have to fight him and give it your all."

After thinking about it all day and night, I made my decision. The next day, the bully approached me again in the street and reminded me that I better not say anything. I told him I would say and do whatever I wanted.

"What?" he asked.

"You heard me!" I said.

"I'll punch you out."

"Try it!"

He took off his jacket and came at me. He hit me in the nose and on my arm. I swung back at him and missed. He hit me again on the head, the front of my chin and missed a couple of times. Blood started to drip out of my nose from that first punch. Seeing the blood, I charged him, swinging wildly. Most of my punches did not find their mark, but one caught his temple. He backed up, but once again came forward and hit me in the jaw and pushed me down. I got up quickly and started swinging at him. I connected at least three times. I was being overwhelmed, but I kept swinging and yelling at him. I connected at least two more times before a couple of adults came by and stopped the fight. My face was swollen, my nose was bleeding and my shirt was torn, but his lip was bruised and swollen and one of his eyes was bloodshot. He definitely got the best of me, but he walked away and never bothered or threatened me again. Whenever I saw him in the street, I would avoid him. His family must have moved not long after that, because I never saw him again.

When I was around eleven or twelve years old, three friends and I started a little calypso band. A guy named Butch and I played bongos. The lead singer played a conga while another fella played sticks and a cow bell. We called ourselves the Mambo Lads. We had a real nice calypso beat. We practiced in our homes and began performing for tips at the corner of 145th Street and 8th Avenue. We really improved over time, and always made enough money to go to the movies or buy sodas, popcorn and candy. Most of time we had money left over to save or share with our parents.

One day after an outstanding performance, a person suggested we look into participating in the amateur night competition at the Apollo. We did and was accepted. Our parents and other relatives and friends came out to support us and I'm proud to say we put on a great show and won the contest.

The managers told us if we won two more times we could perform with the professionals and be paid for at least one week. We were so excited, and practiced day and night. The second week came and once again we were on key. The competition was much keener than the first week, though, and we finished in a tie with a talented female singer. To break the tie, the judge asked the audience to make the final decision by applause. Since we had all our parents and friends in the audience, we won overwhelmingly. With one more win we would be paid for a week's work at the legendary theatre.

We already were earning two to three hundred dollars in tips on Friday and Saturday on the streets and that was big money to us, but we were ecstatic about the chance to earn more. The following Wednesday, with our family

Outside famous Apollo Theatre.

and friends in the audience again, we really turned it on. We had the place jumping - our solos were good, our timing was excellent, and we got a nice ovation. I knew we were in the lead and with only two contestants left our chances of winning seemed pretty good. Two ladies then took the stage. Their performance was good but didn't get the response we got. Then the last contestant came out. He was tall, dark and really handsome. We looked at each other and Butch said, "That don't mean nothing, he's got to have talent." I looked over at some of the female parents and friends and they had their mouths open before he even sang a note.

We wound up taking second place, which paid $50.00. I've often wondered if it was rigged to stop us from winning three in a row. The guy sounded like the great Billy Eckstine. He was just better than us, but we made a lot of people proud.

Now my friends know why I stop and give money to youngsters playing music on the streets before a Pacers or Colts game. It brings back good memories.

Me visiting the Apollo Theatre over 50 years later.

My beginnings in basketball gave no indication of future success in the sport ... not by a long shot. Not even by an easy layup. I constantly double-dribbled and carried the ball. Teammates gave up throwing the ball to me, so shot opportunities were nonexistent. For a long time, I was the last person chosen, always with an, "Aww, all right, I'll take Jerald."

Sure, that hurt. But it might have been the best thing for me. Had I been mediocre instead of terrible I might have been satisfied with that. But, suffering through the humiliation of being the last kid picked ... well, that really hurt.

I kept at it. When I couldn't get playing time on the playgrounds, I worked hard on my own. It's amazing how you can consistently run into a brick wall and then suddenly burst through it. I started to see noticeable improvement in my skills. I was able to control the ball with greater efficiency. And the better I got, the more I wanted to be on the court.

I played basketball day and night, in the rain or light snow. By the time I reached fifth grade in elementary school (P. S. 90, about a half-block from our home), I was one of the first players chosen, usually by the bully kid or his sister. We won almost every game, and not just in basketball. We played touch football, too. I loved sports so much that it became a part of me. It became my identity. Unfortunately, I started to neglect my schoolwork. My mom emphasized academics, but I didn't listen. I did just enough to get by.

One day, to my surprise, the older boys on the block asked me to play basketball with them. I was truly excited, maybe too excited. I bragged so much to my buddies they kicked me out of the block games for a week. They finally relented and asked me to return for their games against the older guys. All was forgiven in the interest of the "greater good."

Basketball also helped me expand my geographic horizons as I started playing against guys in lower Harlem. That's where I learned about organized basketball. I tried out for a team and met the coach who turned out to be one of the great influences on my life, and many others.

Coach Holcombe Rucker taught me the first steps on fundamental basketball. He had set plays, something I hadn't experienced on the playgrounds. One of Rucker's plays was "The Skeleton." I'll never forget it because I kept going the wrong way, but he was patient with me. I kept thinking he was going to cut me, but he never did. I appreciated him then and even more now, because I learned so much about the game at the St. Phillips gym.

Holcomb Rucker, my
first basketball coach.

I ended up playing a supporting role as a starter. The leading players were more developed physically or had started playing the game a year or two ahead of me. We traveled around New York playing against Boys Clubs, the YMCA and the Catholic Youth Organization teams. I don't remember ever losing. Coach Rucker also coached the Midgets, Tots, Juniors and Seniors league teams. As I remember, he always had an even keel about him, never yelling. If anything, he would smile and explain what he was trying to accomplish until you got it. I also do not remember Coach Rucker displaying favoritism, although I'm sure he had his favorites. He was special and saved many young men from going astray.

Holcombe Rucker's legacy lives on in Rucker Park, the Rucker summer league and the prestigious Rucker tournament - yeah, that Rucker.

Born in 1926, Mr. Rucker was an African American educator and coach. From 1948 to 1964 he was the Harlem playground director for the New York City Department of Parks and Recreation. In 1950, he founded a pro-am basketball tournament, which remains one of the most prestigious summer tourneys on the planet. In 1965, the tournament moved from its original location to the P.S. 156 playground at 155th Street and Frederick Douglass Boulevard. In 1974, the city renamed it the Holcombe Rucker Playground. The basketball court at Rucker Park is probably the most famous "street court" in the world.

Some of the greatest basketball players of all time honed their skills in Rucker leagues, Rucker tournaments or pick-up games on Rucker courts. That includes homegrown legends like Connie Hawkins, Roger Brown, Lew Alcindor (Kareem Abdul-Jabbar), Julius "Dr. J" Erving, Nate Archibald and Earl Monroe along with white players from my era ... Billy Cunningham, Larry Brown, Doug Moe, and Donnie Walsh. The list goes on and on. If you were a New York City ballplayer with "game," sooner or later you had to prove it on a Rucker court or in a Rucker tournament or league. Rucker events have also attracted the cream of the crop from other cities.

Philadelphia all-stars regularly flocked to Rucker Park, including Wilt Chamberlain, Guy Rodgers, Hal Lear and Sonny Hill.

Rucker games also helped usher in an exciting new style of basketball. Long before slam dunks and behind-the-back passes were standard fare in the N.B.A., they were commonplace at Rucker.

Through it all, Mr. Rucker stressed education. His motto was, "Each one, teach one." He helped hundreds of youngsters earn basketball scholarships and he set an example by returning to school and graduating from City College of New York (CCNY) with a degree in Education.

There are a number of stories I remember while in P.S. 90 elementary school. The ones that stand out are not necessarily the ones I'm most proud of.

My best friend, Frank Dowell and I had a crush on Gwendolyn Howard in the fifth grade. One day we put together this scheme to trap her in the coat closet and simultaneously kiss her on the cheek. We thought it would be funny and she would get a kick out of it. Well, after we kissed her, she started crying and my teacher, Mrs. Fox, heard her and asked what was going on. We placed our hands together in a praying position, pleading with her not to tell. She responded, "Oh, nothing." We took a deep breath.

The next day, her father came into the classroom to speak to Mrs. Fox. Frank and I were then put in separate corners of the room. We had to stand there all day and miss recess. We were told if that happened again our parents would be called and we would be kicked out of school. I didn't realize until later in life how bad an idea that had been.

Once in the sixth grade, I tried to show off by throwing spit balls in front of some girls during class. My teacher, Mr. Couse, told me to stop. But the girls giggled and I started acting up again. Then Mr. Couse told me to meet him in the hall right outside the classroom. Everybody said in unison, "Oh, Oh!" They knew what that meant, but I couldn't back down in front of the class. Out in the hall, Mr. Couse said, "You know what I have to do?" I said, "Yeah!" And then I felt it, the hardest slap I have ever gotten. The whole class could hear it from the inside with the door closed. My ears started to ring, and then for a minute or so I couldn't hear anything. I entered the classroom trying my best to hide the tears and crack a smile, but it didn't work. Everybody knew I was in pain, and I had a big red mark on my brown face. Mr. Couse couldn't get away with doing that today, but he had very little trouble with the boys he threatened to take into the hall.

Just before leaving elementary school, my teacher told me to study my History and English books because our parents were going to be invited to the classroom to watch us perform. I remember thinking I had to study, but basketball and the calypso band kept interfering.

When Parents' Day came, I wasn't ready. The parents all stood around the class as the teacher began asking questions. Almost everyone was answering their questions correctly. Then the teacher asked me a history question that sounded familiar, so I gave my answer. I wasn't even in the right century. My teacher said, "That's not correct." I looked at my mother, who had a frown on her face.

Only three of the 24 students answered their questions incorrectly, and I was one. The teacher asked us another question and the other two got their questions right. When I got my second turn, you guessed it, I was wrong once again. As the teacher started to ask the class more questions, I snuck another look at my mom and she was looking right back at me with that closed-lip frown on her face. After embarrassing my mother, I began studying more. For a while, anyway. It wasn't long before I went back to my normal ways, doing just enough to get by.

Things were starting to look up as I graduated from elementary school and entered the all-boys Frederick Douglass Junior High (P. S. 139). Clothes and food were no longer an issue thanks to my mother's steady employment and help from family members. Though still basically on the shy side, I was beginning to feel more secure about myself.

I'll say it over and over, I wouldn't trade anything for growing up in Harlem, despite the difficult times. I never drank, smoked or used profanity. I was no angel, but most of my transgressions were mischievous rather than criminal. I can't pin it on any single aspect of my life. Certainly, I had wonderful role models and mentors. My belief is that there was someone watching over me. I won't fall back on the old cliché that "sports saved my life," because I believe I still would have followed the straight and narrow route without any involvement in athletics. Still, while not totally defining me as a person, sports played a major role in shaping my life and pushing me toward a path of success.

I was fortunate to be connected to a number of local individuals and organizations who helped channel my energies and talents through sports. Earlier, I mentioned Holcomb Rucker and the positive influence he had on my life. While it might have seemed no big deal at the time, I remember Olympic middle-distance gold medal winner Mal Whitfield coming to our school. Whitfield won the 800-meter event for the United States in the 1948 and 1952 Olympic Games. Mal passed his track shoes around the assembly hall. I looked closely at the spiked shoes, holding and bending them slightly, before passing them on. I don't remember much about what he said except he was going over to Africa to help the runners there. He also told us to do our best in whatever we did. I really felt good about holding his spikes. Later, my greatest success in track would come in the middle distances ... the 880 and 1,000-yard runs.

There were also organizations that helped me, such as the Police Athletic League (PAL), a non-profit youth development agency whose goal is to promote the prevention of juvenile crime and violence through participation in various activities. Its goal also was to have a good relationship with the community and the police department through positive engagements. In other words, establish an environment in which cops are not conceived as the "bad guys."

While a student at Frederick Douglass, I ran track for the 32nd Precinct of the PAL Club. We didn't have a good team. We didn't have as much talent as some of the other PAL clubs in the area and we had some kids who didn't take the competition as seriously as I did. After one meet at the 369th Armory in Harlem, our coach, a uniformed officer, was extremely angry with us. Mustering up every ounce of courage I had, I approached him - something I would not have dreamed of doing a couple years earlier.

"What do you want?!" he snapped.

"You don't have me entered in the standing broad jump," I said.

He checked his notes and said, "Yeah, okay, get over there."

It was one of the last events of the meet. Without warming up, I jumped far enough to earn a silver medal, unbeknownst to the coach, who was occupied with other duties.

When the meet concluded, the coach waved me over and said, "Come on, let's get out of here."

And, almost as an afterthought, he asked, "How did you do?"

I proudly responded, "Second place," and showed him my medal.

He didn't say a word. Didn't have to. The smile on his face - the first I'd seen all day – said it all. I had won our only team's medal.

Despite my status as "second-fastest kid on the block," I was just above average as a sprinter when it came to competition against other area

PAL Clubs. I was a pretty good standing broad jumper; I won a medal just about every time I competed in my weight group (95 pounds). That silver medal I won in the little PAL meet was, at the time, as precious to me as an Olympic gold medal.

I tried out for the junior high basketball team during my final year and made it, thanks to the fundamentals I learned from Coach Rucker. I was playing more and more and got in for one quarter in the championship game that we lost. I remembered how one of the players got angry at the coach because he didn't play much, so he put the coach's jacket in a pail of water. Again, I was fortunate I never got into serious trouble at P.S. 139 because of good role models such as Roy Phillips, a Frederick Douglass teacher and the PAL coach.

Between playing sports, participating in the calypso band, occasional homework and doing the hambone, I had a full schedule. The hambone was an activity where we used our hands to slap our thighs, chest and sometimes the mouth to make a rhythm beat. I put a lot of time into it and competed against other kids. Every three months or so we would perform on stage during assemblies at Frederick Douglass.

I was voted the best and held the title for more than a year. A new friend of mine followed me around and began copying all my moves. When we competed on stage, the competition was close. I noticed as he performed harder and faster his light-skinned complexion began turning red. Everyone in the audience noticed it and began clapping and cheering really loud, and I wound up losing my title to my so-called friend. I continue to do the hambone to this day, especially when young children are around.

Chapter 5
PATTERSON PROJECTS

I was fifteen when we moved into the Patterson Projects in the Bronx. The first encounter I had was with a group of guys walking toward me on the street. One of them, short and muscular, asked who I was. I told him my name and he said, "You think you're smart. I didn't ask your name and I don't like your looks." He pushed me in the chest, then balled up his fist and moved toward me. I backed up, scared as can be. Then somebody yelled out, "Leave him alone! He ain't bothering anybody." The guy walked toward me and faked a punch, and I jumped back. He laughed, and the group moved on. I went back up to our apartment on the 12th floor to regain my composure.

I finally got my nerve back up and went over to the park, where I saw the same guys playing basketball. I could tell right away I was a better player than any of them. When the game ended, a guy named Junior Grant and the same kid that had saved me from a sure whipping asked me if I wanted to play. I'm a southpaw, but I beat them playing almost single-handedly as a right-handed player. My team stayed on the court the entire day. Afterward, I made friends with my life-saver - his name was Elbert Shamsid-Deen. I asked Deen if the short muscle-bound guy would have fought me. He said, "Yeah! He's always trying to show his toughness because he has problems with his height."

After basketball, we sat on a bench where one of the guys asked me if I wanted some reefer. I said, "Nah." They didn't know I had never even smoked a cigarette. How about a drink? I said, "Nah." The kid responded, "Damn, that's not the way you start a friendship, refusing like that." I just didn't want anything. I noticed that the guys used a lot of profanity, more than my buddies from Harlem. The project cops walked toward us and I knew they had to smell the smoke, but they just talked for five or ten minutes and moved on. As they left one of them said, "I know you guys are going to stay out of trouble. Have a nice night. If you need us, let us know." I found out later that they were not going to harass us on something small like that - especially if they didn't see anything. We got along so well with them. One of the policemen was "Pop" Gates, one of the famous Harlem Globetrotters. We really respected him. Almost all the guys were members of a gang called the Centurions. They said their main purpose was to protect our turf. After my first refusal to join, they suggested I join the Little Centurions, a non-violent group. They could tell from my demeanor I wasn't into all of that. Besides, I was an all-the-way baller, serious about playing sports.

My sister Marlene adjusted easily to the projects. She was well-liked by everybody. She also was a good athlete before she hurt her leg during her teen years.

A lot of different incidents took place while we lived in Patterson. The projects always appeared to me as if they were built right in the middle of an Italian and Irish neighborhood. A small number of kids of those heritages lived inside the projects, along with African Americans, Puerto Ricans and other Hispanic groups. We all hung out together.

One day we heard the news about Emmett Till, a black 14-year-old boy who was beaten to death in Mississippi. His mother wanted an open casket at the funeral so people could see his severely damaged body. Jet magazine published photos of Till. It was a horrendous sight, and black people all over America were livid.

Emmett Till, 14 years old.

There was a luncheonette across the street from the projects where people from the neighborhood and surrounding areas gathered. This particular day, right after people had seen the Emmett Till pictures in Jet magazine, two white teenagers walked out of the store and were immediately approached by at least five members of the project gang, who started yelling "This is for Emmett!" With no warning, they started beating the two boys with their fists. I stood there with my mouth open, and then saw the swelling and blood as they got to their feet and started running. The gang kept hitting them as they ran off. I could still see the anger in the gang members' faces. I thought to myself, why bother them, they weren't the people who killed Emmitt Till? But I knew if I said it out loud, I would be told to shut up before I got popped.

In the summer, a carnival was set up in a surrounding neighborhood. At least 25 guys ran through our projects, jumping on anybody who looked suspicious, in response to the two white guys who had been attacked. I don't know how many they caught to beat, but it was more than two. Then things went back to normal.

Racial tension was everywhere, though. We played basketball teams from nearby neighborhoods at a school called John Peter Zenger (P. S. 18). In one game, we were beating this Irish/Italian team so badly they began hacking us and playing rough. The refs couldn't handle them, so we decided to call for help from the project's community center. Within 15 minutes, about 30 guys walked into the school and surrounded the court. The school director convinced the gang to take their team and small group of followers outside.

One of the project guys came up with the idea of having a one-on-one fight, between an Italian and a black guy, who was dressed in black with black leather gloves. He looked like he could really fight. Right away, they started swinging at each other, with both landing punches. We soon heard sirens, and the police jumped out of their cars and surrounded those of us who didn't get away. I remember my friend Wally started giggling softly as we put our hands on the wall. One of the cops heard him and hit him softly in the head with his billy club. We still laugh at that. After the cops collected the chains and sticks (neither side had guns), they told us to go home and stay out of trouble or we would be sent to jail the next time. After that, it seemed both groups decided to try to get along better. And we did.

Our neighborhood always won the basketball games, though. We had a team called the Clowns, which had been organized a couple of years before I moved into the neighborhood. We weren't very tall, but I learned if you play hard, smart and together you will be surprised what you can accomplish.

The Patterson Project Clowns.

30

I played basketball every day, even by myself in the rain and snow. Eventually, I was named captain of the Clowns. It's hard to put into words how much I loved to play basketball, and how hard I played. I socialized with girls and had my heart broken once or twice, but I got over it because I was going steady with basketball. I loved the game and I loved the competition.

I more than held my own against the older guys in the projects even though they would hack me, knock me down or throw their hats in my face when I shot. I was shorter and weaker than many of them, but still found a way to win. Years later, I realized the benefit of enduring the physical play from those games.

I was tested more in the projects than in Harlem, but I stayed out of trouble because of basketball. I guess that was just my personality, anyway. When I did get into mischief it was small stuff, such as hopping a subway turnstile and riding to go play basketball. One time my Clown friends, Johnny Gibbons, Wally Hassan, Elbert Shamsid-Deen and I were coming back from a game in a taxi, but when we got to the projects they jumped out and ran without paying, I froze, and the cabby took all the pocket change I had. When I saw my buddies, I told them I jumped out but ran in another direction. I was so upset with the guys, I started running with a more diverse group, Alvin Reed, Ronald Green and others. They were younger and a little more clean-cut. We played sports together and enjoyed each other's company, but something was missing and I always ended up returning to Deen, Wally, Johnny and others. I just learned to pick the situations I needed to avoid. They tried to get me to smoke, but I refused because I thought it would harm my athletic career. While playing card games like Whist, I got a contact high because all the guys around me were smoking reefer. Everything was spinning around in my head and I got a bad headache. The guys just laughed at me, but I was too dizzy to understand why.

Thunderbird liquor was also popular at the time. The slogan went, "What's the word? Thunderbird! What's the price? Thirty twice!" I never drank because of sports and I could not stand the idea that my mother might catch me drinking or smell the booze on my breath. I never cursed, either. When I got really mad I would say, "mother fletcher." My friends would shout, "That's a curse! Jerry cursed!" I would say, "No it isn't!"

One time I was sitting on a bench with some friends and a guy snuck up behind me and held me while holding a handkerchief with something in it over my nose. I started screaming and yelling. All the guys burst out laughing and once again my best buddy Elbert said, "Leave him alone, that's not right! Why did you do that?" They all kept laughing, including Deen. To this day I don't know what was in that handkerchief. They said it was ammonia. I guess I was a geek who just wanted to play sports with a healthy body and clear head.

There was diversity within my Patterson Projects friends. That's me in the second row left next to Ronald Green with glasses. I bet 95% of these guys were winners in their walk in life.

One thing about my street buddies, they always had your back. They were like my brothers. Here's a good example. I liked my mother's boyfriend, Al, because he treated my mom well. But one day they had a small spat, which bothered me. I went down the elevator to the street and immediately ran into Deen, Johnny and Wally, along with other Centurions. They could see I was a little upset. They asked what was wrong, and I finally told them my mother's boyfriend had made me upset. They said, "What? You want us to go up there and give him a beating?" I said "Nah, it's not like that." I had to hold those guys back. I am sure they would have hurt him badly. They said "If you ever have any more problems with that fool let us know, we'll take care of it." And they meant it.

The projects were ours and everything in it belonged to us. I remember the time three guys came into Patterson to visit some of our ladies they had met shopping on 149th and 3rd Avenue. They were nicely dressed, and handsome. The girls were truly impressed, giggling and whispering to each other on the project bench. After the guys walked the girls to their building entrance and started home, about 10 of us walked toward them. We just told them, "We don't want to ever see you in our projects again! This is a warning this time, there will be consequences next time." They looked at us, nodded their heads and kept walking.

Would you believe they had the nerve to try to sneak back into Patterson to see the girls? We surrounded the three of them. They started pleading, but it was too late. We started beating and hitting them with our fists, chains and sticks. The girls started screaming and yelling, which brought the project police to the scene as we ran away. The guys were a little bloody and swollen, but it could have been worse. The girls liked the idea that we cared enough to fight for them – as a matter fact, they were elated. And oh, by the way, we never saw those guys in Patterson again.

Chapter 6
THE DEWITT CLINTON EXPERIENCE

In my freshman year at DeWitt Clinton High, I went out for the track team late in the season. Our first meet was at the Fort Washington Avenue Armory between 168th and 169th Street. I had only practiced a little bit, but I was still feeling so confident I asked to run the anchor leg of the 1200-yard relay team. I had never run 300 yards but what the heck? Plus, there were girls in the stands from our neighbor school, Walton High, who were cheering for us. I got the baton in last place, but within striking distance. The five runners in front of me were all boxed up with about 200 yards to go.

The first-place runner tripped and fell, taking down the other four runners with him. Suddenly, I was running in first-place with a grin on my face. I could hear the cheering from the stands as I approached the half-way mark, but all of a sudden, my legs began to wobble. I felt as though I was carrying somebody on my shoulders. I looked back, and the five guys who had fallen were about 15 yards behind me. I tried to push a little harder, but it wasn't helping. My PAL coach had told me not to look back, to just keep running, but my curiosity got the best of me. I could see their faces pretty clearly. They were about five yards back now. I panicked and started to strain, but I had nothing left. With about 20 yards to go, all five runners were now neck-and-neck with me. I said to myself, there must be something left in my body, please! The answer was no. All five runners went by me and pulled away. I was wobbling and dizzy as I crossed the finish line, and finally fell down.

When I looked up I saw three runners with their hands on their hips. Another guy had his hands on his head and the final guy had his hands on his knees. I wondered for a second, did I beat them? Then reality set in, the five guys that had tripped over each other had beaten me to the finish line. My buddy Frank Dowell ran over and asked if I was all right. I said "Yeah, but could you do me a favor? Get my clothes and bag and bring them to me under the stands. I don't feel like going up there." He told me the guys and girls from school were cheering for me, but I told him I didn't want to go back up into the stands to get my bag and have to answer their questions. I asked Frank to take my baton to the coach, too.

When Frank returned with my clothes, I asked if the coach had asked for me. He said no, he was trying to get another relay team together, but was glad to get the baton. I took the subway home, but on the way, I felt sorry for myself. I wasn't that bad of a guy, I thought, and here it was getting close to Christmas. I thought I deserved better than to be embarrassed in front of my friends. I also was worried that Lilly, one of the girls who came to the track meet, would tell people in the Patterson what happened. I was so relieved that it was Friday and I wouldn't have to go to school the next day.

CROSS COUNTRY, TRACK AND FIELD TEAMS—MR. C. SCHER

DeWitt Clinton 1958 track team. I'm 4th from left in the top row. 4th from right is Gary Gubner who held the shot-putt world record. We both got gold medals in the city track and field championship. Coach Charlie Scher, middle, second row (in suit) never gave up on me until I succeeded. *Photo courtesy Clinton Athletics.*

On Monday the track coach, Charlie Scher, saw me in the hall between classes and asked where have you been? I told him I was unhappy about not doing well. He said, "What do you expect, you haven't hardly practiced at all! You cannot just go out there and succeed without putting forth the effort. It's just like everything else in life, you have to work for it. The harder you work, the better your chances of reaching your goal."

I took the coach's words to heart. I began working out on my start, leg lift, form, baton passing and leaning into the tape at the finish. After a couple of weeks of practice, I felt I was ready. I had grown a couple of inches over the summer to 6 foot-1 ½ and I had worked hard. I felt really confident about my first 100-yard dash. Two of the guys in my heat, Calvin Barnes and Freddie Macon, lived in my neighborhood and I had always beaten them. I also was running in lane 3, a good place to see your competitors on each side.

We were running on a cinder track at Macombs Park, right across from Yankee Stadium. I was familiar with it. Wearing my black and red Clinton uniform, I was ready. I thought I was off to a good start after the gun went off, but at the 30-yard mark I was in fifth place. Two of the guys I always beat in the neighborhood were leading. I moved into fourth place with 20 yards to go and then told myself, It's now or never! I gave it all I had and leaned into the tape in fourth place. The two runners I usually beat were overjoyed over finally beating me. I hadn't even advanced to the semifinal heat.

When I reached the stands coach Scher said, "Not bad, that's your best time in the 100." I didn't care about my time, I had finished fourth and I had lost to those two guys for the first time. The coach said, "Jerald, you even said yourself, that you had grown three inches, you no longer take quick short steps." I didn't want to hear that. I went home and decided I was wasting my time. I was going to quit.

I ducked coach Scher all week, but he finally found me in gym class and asked why I hadn't been at practice.

I said, "Coach, I didn't know how to tell you, but I decided to quit."

"You make it a habit of quitting on yourself, don't you?" he said.

I shrugged my shoulders and went back to shooting baskets. He started to walk away, but then yelled back to me, "Hey you know, you had a nice stride in the 100-yard run. Why don't you start practicing with the distance runners?" I looked up and saw about 15 guys, only one of them black, running together around the oval track that circled the upper level of the gym. "That's for the white guys," I said to myself and went back to shooting baskets.

After a couple of weeks of going home after school and watching television, doing homework and having dinner, I started missing the guys - the laughter, the camaraderie and running together in the uniforms. I decided to go back. coach Scher didn't get angry, he just asked if I was going to run with the distance runners. I hadn't thought about it, so I said yes. I ran toward the back of the group at first, but after a month I was running in the middle. After another month I was one of the top five runners on the team. And by the end of the season I was one of the five fastest 880-yard runners in the Bronx.

I began running cross country as a sophomore and learned to enjoy the 2 ½-mile races. As a junior, I won the Bronx championship in cross country and finished in the top 15 in the New York City cross country championship meet.

I had found my place in track and field, all because I hadn't quit and more importantly, coach Scher stayed on me.

I started practicing my distance running in the projects on the weekend and continued playing basketball with the Clowns at P.S. 18. I also participated in an intramural program at Clinton. My classroom won the intramural championship and I scored 24 of our team's 27 points.

Everyone was suggesting I go out for the varsity basketball team, but I wasn't confident I could make the team, and I didn't want to be disappointed. I was doing well in track and I enjoyed playing with the Clowns in evenings and on the weekends, so I was getting my fill of basketball.

Still, during the summer before my senior year I was thinking of going out for the Clinton varsity team. I went over to the Harlem Y one morning to shoot around as I usually did. I begged the staff to let me in for free because I didn't have the 25-cent admission fee. I was let in, but with a warning that I would have to have a pass or money the next time. I was shooting around when I heard a voice behind me say something like, "You know, you're not that bad. Keep it up!" When I turned to thank him, my mouth flew open and my eyes bulged out. I was shocked. I had seen him before because he was often there talking to the Y director and some of the other boys, but never this close.

It was Jackie Robinson. Yes, *that* Jackie Robinson.

In my senior year, I once again captured the Bronx cross country championship at Van Cortlandt Park by some ten yards. Right away, I began preparing for the city championship, which included about 400 runners.

My strategy was to get out fast over the quarter-mile flat field at the start of the course so I wouldn't get tangled up in traffic. When I reached the hills, I was among the top 20 runners, and then 15. I thought maybe I'd started too quickly, because the course was difficult, and so was the competition. I fell back into the top 25 runners, where I was bumped around some coming off the hill and entering a narrow straight-away. After running about a mile, the saliva in my mouth started to thicken and I wondered if I could go another mile-and-a-half at this pace.

I moved back into the top 20 with a mile to go. I kept telling myself my second wind would be kicking in soon, and that I was better than most of the other runners. I passed a group of five going into a soft sandy area. My mouth was really dry at this point, but I kept passing runners. I was moaning with pain as I told myself to kick into another gear. I moved up to the top 10. We then came out of a clump of trees near the highway, about 200 yards from the path to the finish line. I could feel the second wind kicking in as I passed three other runners to move into seventh place. Entering the final straight-away, a quarter mile from the finish line, I could hear the cheering. I started sprinting past four runners while telling myself, I can do it! With 100 yards to go I was about 10 yards behind a guy name Richard Kier. The first-place runner, Tom Laris, had crossed the finish line. I was hoping to get Kier, who was now five yards ahead of me. I set myself up to pass him on the right. I knew I didn't have much in the tank and Kier moved to his right to block me. I tried to go around him, but he moved over again and again. With spectators to my right, my only choice was to cut back to his left side and try to pass, but I had been thrown off-stride and couldn't do it. I settled for third place.

I knew I was a better runner than him, but he had out-maneuvered me. Kier went on to become a good runner at the University of Nebraska and Laris became a member of the U.S. Olympic team. My future, though, was going to be in another sport. Jackie Robinson's few words had inspired me to try out for the Clinton basketball team.

I surprised myself in the tryouts for the basketball team, but still wasn't sure if I was good enough. Most of the guys from the previous season's team were from another part of town, and I assumed they were better than me. I wondered if the coach, Hank Jacobson, would favor those players. I wondered if I was shooting well enough and playing good defense. I was a distance run-ner, so I wondered if I was fast enough for basketball. Making matters worse, I didn't know most of the other guys that well, so I felt like an outsider, too.

I worried every time the list of players who had survived the previous cut was posted. Then, finally, it came down to the 12 players who would be on the team. I knew I hadn't had a good scrimmage the day before, so I was really worried. I tossed and turned all night before the fateful day, hardly able to sleep. Then, I was looking at the list and running my finger down to the letter H but couldn't find my name. I was devastated, but quickly woke up and shook off the nightmare.

When I got to school I immediately ran to the list and found my name. I was thrilled, but I wondered why it wasn't in alphabetical order. One of the players, Popcorn Ferguson, came by and I asked him. "They never put it in alphabetical order," he said. "You must have been dreaming." He didn't know how right he was.

Our first preseason scrimmage was against Wingate High, in our gym. I didn't start but played half of the game. They beat us on a last-second shot by a sophomore named Roger Brown, who played center. I remember thinking, *Is the competition that good? That Brown guy is really impressive.* I continued

1958 City Champs, DeWitt Clinton Basketball team. I'm number 77. Coach Hank Jacob in the second-row left was fighting for his job, he won it when we captured the 1958 City Basketball Championship with a 52-41 score over Boys High.
Photo courtesty DeWitt Clinton Sports.

to play well in scrimmages and practice and worked my way into the starting lineup by the time the season began. We won our first five games before losing to Forest Hill on the road, 61-51, and was 8-2 at the Christmas break, losing also to Morris High.

Our first opponent in the Public-School Athletic League City Championship at Madison Square Garden was Lincoln High. We won, 65-54, but I was nervous and only scored six points. I scored 16 points in the second game, a 62-46 victory over Music and Art, and then we met Morris High again. They were up by 10 at halftime and by 12 going into the final period.

I will never forget coach Jacobson crying as he talked to us before the start of the fourth quarter. Tears were falling as he shouted at us: "We can win this game! Please, please, we have to reach deep down!" We came out in a full court press that sent us on a 10-point spree. The game went into overtime, and I hit all five of my free throw shots to help secure the win, 59-57. I set a New York high school record for the Garden in that game, hitting all 14 foul shots. We were now in the finals against heavily favored Boys High.

During pre-game warmups I watched them put on a dunking show, led by Billy Burwell, their 6'10" center who took two basketballs and dunked them one after the other. Their forward, Jackie Jackson, executed a turn-around dunk and a guard, Jerry Powell, was hitting long jumpers. I thought, Oh, my, that's enough. I told my teammates not to look.

Amazingly enough, one of our reserves, Alvin Reid, came off the bench early in the second half and hit some crucial long shots to give us a lead we never relinquished. Our defense, led by Les Coleman, Charlie Fowler and Popcorn Ferguson was superb, and we won, 52-41. I led the team with 14 points. We also woke up a sleeping giant, a freshman on the Boys High bench who was in tears after the loss: a kid named Connie Hawkins.

And to think I had decided to go out for the team only because Jackie Robinson had given me a mild compliment at the Harlem Y. (Incidentally, Wally, Deen and I went by the Y 55 years later and the name had been changed. It's now called the Jackie Robinson Youth YMCA.)

My first favorite Brooklyn Dodger had been Duke Snider, who batted left-handed like me, and then it was Gil Hodges, who played first base like me. I remember folding up my short-sleeved shirt like Hodges, despite my skinny arms. Finally, Jackie became my favorite. I idolized him, because I realized what he stood for.

Deen, myself, and Wally visited the Harlem YMCA 55 years later.

Jackie has rightfully received credit for a lot of accomplishments, but not enough for his mentoring. He talked with and tried to motivate young black boys like me at the Y. He also brought two of his Dodger teammates, catcher Roy Campanella and pitcher Don Newcome, to talk to us. I admired his knowledge of baseball, his hustle and how he responded to questions from the Knot Hole Gang on the radio. I was so impressed I even started imitating his pigeon-toed walk.

After helping Clinton win the city basketball title, I started training for track and field. I wasn't in peak distance running form, but at least was in shape from basketball. It didn't take long to change my training focus and I went on to easily win the 1000-yard run by five yards in the Bronx championship meet.

When the city track and field championship at Randalls Island rolled around, I felt I was ready. Maybe too ready. I warmed up too hard and for too long because some of the guys came on the field to tell me coach said to slow down. I just looked at them and smiled. I thought I knew what I was doing. I got out at my normal pace and was in the top five in a field of 24. At the quarter-mile mark, I was among the top three. I took the lead with two hundred yards to go. But with 50 yards to go, I was really huffing and puffing. Tom McGrath, my toughest opponent, and two others passed me. I concentrated and caught up with McGrath while the other two fell behind. We were neck-and-neck. McGrath took the lead with 10 yards to go, but I gave it everything I had and passed him for the win and the gold medal.

I was excited but exhausted. I made my way to the infield and fell down. After catching my breath, I looked up and there stood the basketball star Roger Brown, who had just won the high jump title. He showed me his gold medal and said "You know, you are almost killing yourself out here. I just jump over a bar, and we get the same medal." He smiled and added, "You know, I feel sorry for you." And then he laughed and walked away.

(Fifty-five years later, while researching information for this book, I discovered Richard Kier was in the race that I won. It was a great feeling, knowing I had gotten revenge from the cross country race earlier that year.)

Later in the year, I was named the DeWitt Clinton High School Athlete of the Year, my first major individual honor.

I've always felt close to Clinton. I attended a 50th-year reunion in the Bronx, where I was able to reconnect with entertainer Robert Klein, who I believe had been the student body vice-president, and Eddie Lewis, who had been the captain of the Clinton football team and went on to be a co-founder of Essence magazine.

As my senior year at Clinton neared its end, my athletic accomplishments were growing, and I was feeling good about my chance of getting a college athletic scholarship. I had just captured the 1,000-yard run at the outdoor City Championship. I had finished third out of 400 boys in the cross-country City Championship meet. I was one of the top scorers on the basketball team that won the city championship, and I was voted second-team All-City along with Roger Brown and Fred Crawford, both of whom went on to play professionally.

I heard St. John's was interested in me for track, but nobody from the university contacted me. Apparently, I had taken the wrong classes. For example, I took algebra and general math but no calculus, geometry or trigonometry. My grade point average didn't help: 2.1 on a 4-point scale. I also didn't have enough hours to get my general diploma, much less an academic diploma. I got a "D" in one of my key subjects and needed a C to graduate. I was told to take another class in the summer and, if I passed, I'd get my diploma.

I also started playing in summer league basketball. Howie Garfinkel, the legendary scout who later co-founded the Five-Star Basketball Camp, asked me to play on his team. We won all our games up to the finals, where we faced the Gems, a team boasting talent such as future professional stars Roger Brown, Connie Hawkins and Larry Brown. We lost a close game, but I scored more than 20 points. We did get revenge the following year, beating them with a host of freshmen college players including Tony Jackson and LeRoy Ellis from St. John's and Barry Kramer and Ray Paprocky from NYU. I didn't start but played good minutes.

New York University basketball coach Lou Rossini told me he was impressed with my game and asked me if I was working. When I told him I wasn't, he said he knew of a firm that was looking for help. I applied and got a nice summer job. With the ball-playing and working, I decided to take just one summer school subject. I passed and got my diploma, but it was too late to march with my class at commencement.

DeWitt Clinton 50 year reunion. I joined entertainer Robert Klein and former co-owner of Essence Magazine, Ed Lewis.

Photo courtesy Henry Ordosgoitia, DeWitt Clinton High School.

Chapter 7
LIFE CHANGER

Then came a life-changing experience. Walter November, a local insurance broker and neighborhood basketball coach, asked me to play on his summer team, the Reliables. When Mr. November asked me if I had a college commitment, I had to tell him the unfortunate truth: I hadn't committed to a college because no college had been willing to commit to me.

"Let's work on that" he said.

November contacted Bridgeport College in Connecticut and arranged for a tryout for my Clowns teammate Elbert Shamsid-Deen and me. We played well against Bridgeport's varsity squad, but nothing came of it. November told me it was due to my grades.

Around that time, I heard from Texas Southern University, a predominantly African American school in Houston that had placed third in the 1958 NAIA basketball tournament. Texas Southern sent me the school's yearbook and showed considerable interest, even though the coaches there had not seen me play. New York University coach Lou Rossini also called and told me to take the entrance exam for that school.

Suddenly, things were looking up.

The following week, however, a representative from Texas Southern called and told me the athletic dormitory had burned down. I would have to wait until next year to enroll. Not another semester, another year. I was heartbroken, especially when I went back through the Texas Southern yearbook and saw the pictures of all those beautiful young ladies.

I still had interest from NYU, which had helped me get a job. A week after hearing the bad news from Texas Southern, coach Rossini called. I felt encouraged hearing his voice, and he told me to come to his office. My mom had a big smile on her face as I packed a suitcase and left to take the subway to campus. I thought to myself, "I am going to play with 'Satch' Sanders, Cal Ramsey and Russ Cunningham. Wow!" They had been the nucleus of NYU's 1960 Final Four team.

After receiving directions to coach Rossini's office, he sat me down and made some small talk – and then informed me I did not pass the entrance exam.

"You got to be kidding me!" was about the only thing I could think to say.

Rossini went on to say, "Your boss wants to thank you, though, for the nice job you did at work and wishes you well. I had hoped to have better news. I am so sorry."

I thanked him for the opportunity and dragged that even-heavier suitcase back to the subway, and then across six blocks back to the projects. When I reached the 12th floor in the smelly elevator in our building, my mother was waiting in the hallway. She could tell from my face something was wrong. When I told her I hadn't been admitted, she said not to worry. She had no doubt that I was going to make it somewhere.

"But Mom, nobody wants me," I said.

She reminded me of all she had been through to find steady work. I had no answer to that. I wish I had hugged and kissed her, but I just grinned at her and walked away.

Thank God for my mother, I thought. She had just gotten another job closer to the projects, putting together rhinestone jewelry, and had overcome a lot of hardships in her life. How could I give up?

One day this guy looked me up at our apartment in the projects and asked me to step out into the hallway. He introduced himself and told me he had a proposition for me, one that would pay me $3,000.

He asked if I knew Bernard Cabey from Toledo University and Wayne Davis from the University of Connecticut, both graduates of DeWitt Clinton. I said yes, although I didn't know them that well. Then he made an offer: "I want you to contact Wayne and ask him to help. Connecticut is favored to win by 12 points in an upcoming game at the Garden. If he could take it easy and his team wins by six points, we all win. Now keep in mind, we want Connecticut to win, but by less than 12 points. If that happens, you get $3,000 dollars, and he would, too. It's time for you to turn things around in your life. There is more to come after that, a lot more."

"Wow! I'm going down there," I said.

"Good!" he said. "I'm staying at the Hilton Hotel and you can reach me there."

I jumped on the subway that afternoon and headed for the hotel near Madison Square Garden where Wayne was staying. But on the way, I started thinking. It just didn't sound right. Was it against the law? We certainly could use the money, especially now that I didn't have a summer job. After considerable thought, I got off the subway, walked to the other side of the platform, and took the train home. I had decided not to contact Wayne.

I lounged around the next two weeks, feeling down and out. Why didn't I work harder in my studies? Why didn't the coaches at Clinton point me in the right direction? Was it their responsibility? It all pointed back to me. I had been told of the importance of my classroom performance. My advisor wasn't sure if I wanted to go to college. She didn't even know I was in sports. I was on the right track to graduate and that was her goal, but not to go to college.

Early that spring, after sitting out the school year, I got another offer. Bowling Green of Ohio offered me a partial scholarship, with the promise it would become a full ride if I played well and stayed eligible. I had no money to pay for anything, so that was a no at the start.

I started playing in outdoor leagues again that summer. Once again, I played really well, and there was an added sense of desperation to my game now. I was like a hungry man facing a nearly-empty plate of food.

We finally got some good news.

After my last game with Walter November's Reliables team, he said to me, "I don't want to get your hopes up, but I'm talking again with coach George Ireland from Loyola of Chicago. He came to see you play when you had a bad game."

I remembered. It was the first game in the City Tournament at Madison Square Garden against Lincoln. I played poorly and scored only six points in our 65-54 win.

"I told Ireland you were a diamond in the rough," November said. "And that you're a good kid who could do much better in the classroom. You just needed a chance."

"What did he say to that?" I asked.

"He said he'd get back to me," November said.

November called me two days later and said Ireland was coming to town for other business the following week and wanted to talk with me and my mother at our home. Once again, November told me not to get my hopes up. I asked him if Ireland knew about my grades.

"Yes," November said. "But he also knows about your good character and your determination to do better."

Finally, the day came ... the meeting with the head basketball coach from Loyola of Chicago, my mom and me. A star player for Notre Dame in the 1930s, Ireland had been Loyola's head coach since the 1951-52 season. He was extremely cordial, especially to my mom. In fact, he didn't speak much to me. It was almost as if he was recruiting her to come to Loyola. He complimented her every opportunity he got. I suspected he knew this was probably my last chance for college, but he acted as if I had a hundred offers. He told my mom that his first goal was to get me through college with a degree. He told her he would look after me like a father, and that basketball would be the last thing on his mind in terms of my success.

"I have some fine things in store for your son," he told her.

He showed her pictures of the new dorm where I would be living and the Loyola campus, with Lake Michigan in the background.

He finally said, "We do hope you'll pick Loyola as your choice for your son. It was a pleasure meeting you. And young man, good luck to you."

Ireland saw my mother's smile before he left, but not her tears after he was gone. I called November right away. He was happy for me. I could tell he already knew Loyola was going to take a chance on me.

"The rest is up to you now," he said.

I was elated. Finally, my opportunity had arrived. My mother and I cried tears of joy.

Coach George Ireland.
Courtesy Loyola Chicago Athletic Department.

Chapter 8
LIFE AT LOYOLA

Art McZier, a recently-graduated black Loyola star, met me at the Chicago airport. McZier may have been responsible for the most memorable moment in Loyola basketball history up to that time. During his senior season, he hit a last-second shot to give the Ramblers a 57-56 win over a great Kentucky team at Chicago Stadium.

"Once you find your way, you are going to be just fine," he said.

McZier dropped me off at the dormitory. I was impressed. The front desk and lounge area were new and spacious, and my room was very nice. The next day I met with coach Ireland, who took me to the office of Harry L. McCloskey, the dean of students.

Ireland started the conversation by telling him how good the team was going to become with me on it. I was shocked to hear that. I started to butt in with, "It takes a team effort to win," but I thought better of it. Ireland finally got around to the main subject: my grades. Ireland assured the dean I was willing to work hard in the classroom to make the grade. Ireland's eyes met mine, a signal for me to speak up.

I told Dean McCloskey that I greatly appreciated him for giving me this chance of a lifetime and I promised not to let him or my mother down. I told the dean I planned to work harder on my schoolwork than basketball, at least until I adjusted to college academics. I went on to say I would discipline myself to put more emphasis on my grades than a social agenda.

I could tell Dean McCloskey was impressed, but he also established the ground rules.

"You will be on probation," he said. "If you don't start making the grades, there will be no hesitation. I wish you the best. Your life's success will depend on what you do these next few years. Ireland then drove me back to the dorm after visiting the three thousand-seat gymnasium. He told me I could go there to shoot at any time.

McZier, who was still playing amateur ball in the area, later picked me up at the dorm to play basketball at Northwestern University against some of their varsity players. I was surprised at how well I did. Willie Jones, Sup Campbell, and Ralph Wells were on hand. On another occasion, I played in a pickup game with a high school player who was better defensively than any of the centers I had played against in New York. His name was George Wilson. We won every game easily. The next time I would meet George Wilson was as an opponent. Meanwhile, McZier began telling everyone how good he thought I was going to be. It gave me needed confidence.

My roommate was a teammate named Clarence Red, who turned out to be a great mentor. Clarence was a pre-dental major, just as nice and clean-cut as they come. Early on, he told me I was at a huge disadvantage, but I could make it. What put me at a disadvantage? "Your study habits," he said.

He explained that I needed to learn how to study, what to study and how much to study. When some of the guys came by to go play ball, he would remind me, "Don't you have a history quiz coming up? Or an English test?" He didn't want anybody else in our room when he was studying, and he told me it was only going to get harder. It wasn't what I wanted to hear, but what I needed to hear.

As I look back, he was the perfect roommate for me.

Clarence Red might have been a perfect mentor for me, but I wasn't anything close to a perfect pupil. Bad habits are hard to break. I knew I was on scholastic probation and I thought I understood what that entailed, but the full meaning of it didn't fully register with me.

I spent considerable time at the gym and not enough time with my studies. I should have followed Clarence's lead. He got it done both on and off the court. Looking back, I think he and his potential influence was a major reason coach Ireland took a chance on me. A product of Landry High School in the Algiers sector of New Orleans, Clarence was entering his junior year when he and I first roomed together. Clarence came to Loyola as a perimeter player, but Coach Ireland converted him to center, even though he had never played the pivot position with his back to the basket.

At 6-foot-6, Clarence was an undersized center but you wouldn't know it by his results. All he did as a sophomore was lead Loyola in scoring (20.3 points-per-game) and rebounding (16.8 rpg). In fact, he led Loyola in rebounding all three of his varsity seasons. He not only studied through the week, but on weekends, too. *The weekend?* I thought that was prime time for socializing. Clarence kept reminding me to hit the books and I kept saying,

"I will, I will." My prophetic roommate, a future dentist, informed me that when I finally decided to buckle down it might be too late.

Don't misunderstand. I didn't completely blow off my studies. But the couple evenings per week that I put into it wasn't nearly enough, especially for someone with my academic background. The other side of college life – the social side – was a different story. The temptation of hanging out with the guys in their rooms was just too much. At the time, freshmen couldn't play varsity ball so playing pickup games with the varsity players was an enjoyable diversion from the books, especially because I played pretty well against them. Going out for pizza, playing whist, and attending parties on Chicago's South Side with my new friend, freshman teammate Herman Hagen, also provided pleasant distractions from the business at hand. The South Side parties were especially difficult to pass up, as they made for a blossoming social life. Girls seemed to like me more in college than in the projects. I liked one in particular, but they all were very impressive.

I was in heaven - or so I thought - as I took advantage of practically every social opportunity. But as you've probably guessed, I paid the price. I was unprepared for my mid-term exams. I wouldn't get the official results until after the holidays but I knew they would not be good.

I called my mom and informed her of the situation. Her reply was short, not-so-sweet, but oh, so true: "You can do it if you want it. I have to go now." And she hung up the phone.

Tough love.

The holiday break also represented a break from basketball. I took the money from my laundry stipend and purchased a round-trip bus ticket from Chicago to New York, not even sure if I'd be able to use the return portion.

It was the longest trip of my life, and not just because of the 16-hour bus ride. My mood shifted from depression to anxiety and back again. I thought of all the people I had let down, including coach Ireland, Walter November, Maurice Phillip and Holcombe Rucker. Most of all, I had disappointed my mother. She was so proud that I made it to college. It probably was as much her dream as mine.

My mood picked up upon seeing my family and friends back home, even more so when November produced a pair of tickets for me and my friend, Elbert Shamsid-Deen, to attend the Madison Square Holiday Festival. I still wanted to *watch* college basketball even if I was unsure that I'd still be *playing* it.

That final night consisted of a triple-header. St. Bonaventure played St. John's and St. Joseph's played NYU in the first two games, but there was no doubt about the marquee game: the championship contest between unbeaten Cincinnati and a strong Iowa team that featured future National Basketball Association player and coach Don Nelson. To be more specific, Elbert and I – and most of The Garden crowd – were there primarily to see Cincinnati's marvelous Oscar Robertson.

Oscar was a genuine superstar. In high school, he led Indianapolis Crispus Attucks to Indiana state championships in 1955 and 1956, marking the first time an all-black school won an open state championship anywhere in the country. In his first two varsity seasons at Cincinnati, he led the nation in scoring and was named the college Player of the Year for each one.

He also made Madison Square Garden his personal showcase. As a sophomore, 10 games into his collegiate career, he set a Garden record by scoring 56 points in Cincinnati's 118-54 victory over Seton Hall despite being taken out of the game with 2 minutes, 46 seconds remaining. That's right. He personally outscored the opposing team. As a junior, Oscar returned to the Garden and torched NYU for 45 points despite the defensive efforts of NYU stars Satch Sanders and Cal Ramsey. And now, after scoring 72 points combined in Cincinnati's first two games of the Holiday Festival, Oscar was going to play in the championship game. And I was going to be there to see it.

Although my memory is a bit hazy, I remember that Elbert and I brushed by Robertson at some point prior to the championship game. He already had on his game face, like a gladiator preparing for battle. Elbert and I were in awe of him ... *before* the game. You see those eyes?

Despite that, and despite all the hype surrounding Robertson, he *exceeded* expectations. He scored a tournament-record 50 points to lead Cincinnati's victory over Iowa. Impressive, yes, but it was how he did it that made a lasting impression on me. He got all of his teammates involved. Triple-double? The term wasn't in use then, but he achieved them routinely. He was a complete player who scored, rebounded and passed to his teammates, like nobody before him.

Elbert and I cheered, laughed and jumped up and high-fived each other the entire game. We were in tears watching this master of the hardcourt.

"Did you see that shot from the corner? Was he out of bounds?"

"How about that dish to his teammate for the easy score!"

"I didn't know he was that quick."

"I didn't know he was that strong."

I was so inspired by Robertson's performance that it rejuvenated me. It made another connection for me. I thought to myself, *You've got to make it, I have to hit the books.*

Oscar Robertson, The Big "O".
Courtesy Crispus Attucks Museum

I re-dedicated myself to succeeding on the court and in the classroom.

Of course, there still was the matter of convincing the folks back at Loyola, including the no-nonsense Jesuits. When I got back to school, my grade card confirmed my fears: Four Ds and Two Cs.

Coach Ireland called me to his office.

"You are inches away from going home," he informed me. "As a matter of fact, I had to fight to stop them from kicking you out. It's all up to you now."

It was more than a wake-up call. It was as if a brass band was blaring "Reveille" in my ears. Here was a coach who had stuck his neck out for me, who had assured the Dean of Students, with me sitting right next to him, that this kid from New York – with a poor academic record – had the grit and determination to succeed. And here I was, clinging to a final thread.

Unfortunately, it takes some people – like a young Jerry Harkness – a long time to learn not to self-destruct. Today I tell youngsters, "Outsiders will throw enough obstacles in your way. Why create your own? There's no shame in not achieving all of your goals. You'll win some, you'll lose some. But if you give it your best shot, there's no disgrace. Learn from your mistakes; don't repeat them."

Fortunately, I survived my irresponsibility. Finally, I got it.

The academics weren't easy for me but I worked at them. I started studying six to seven days a week. I never missed a class. If I had a question, I called my professor at home. I asked if I could do extra work. I participated in the classroom discussion. When I had a question or knew an answer, I would blurt it out and then have to apologize for talking before being called on.

My grades for the next semester were two B's, two C's and one D - not exactly Rhodes Scholar material, but a major improvement. I had earned it. In English I was battling for a C and stayed up all night preparing for a 100-word spelling test. I got a 94 and got my C for the course.

I was happy about the semester results and so was coach Ireland. However, my trouble did not end there.

One Friday evening during the second semester, I was visiting the Carroll family on the South Side of Chicago. I had a great deal of admiration for the Carroll's. They were a beautiful family, with a mother *and* father together. Sure, I'll admit I especially liked one of the three daughters, but I enjoyed the company of the entire family.

On this occasion we got into a deep discussion about civil rights and politics and I forgot I had to be back at the dorm before midnight. I rushed back on the elevated train and got to the school around 12:40 a.m. The door to the dorm was locked at 12 o'clock on the weekend and 11 p.m. during the week. I hit a window with a pebble and asked Herman Hagan to let me in. I sneaked into my room and went to bed. But the dormitory administrator, a priest, came in while I was half-asleep and had me sign a letter which, unknown to me, stated I had arrived late to the dorm. The next morning, I was told I had to leave the dormitory for violating rules. Ireland was able to delay my move until Monday night, which gave him time to find me a place in Evanston. I went to live with the family of Jim Dawson, a Loyola player.

I matured a great deal as a result of this situation. I had to get up early to catch the bus to go to class. I couldn't study in the dorm. I studied in the gym between classes, and then back to the gym for practice. After my meal in the cafeteria, I had to rush to catch the bus to Evanston. That was my routine the entire semester. It probably helped my grades because I had nothing to do but study at the Dawson home. I learned to budget my time, and the family members kept reminding me not to mess up my opportunity.

Basketball was going well, though. I averaged 23 points per game and led the freshmen team to an 8-1 record. Our only loss was to the Jamaco Saints, an excellent amateur team that included Art McZier.

Challenges remained, however. One day late in my freshman season coach Ireland yelled at me during practice. I had no idea why. My grades were good and I had earned my way back into the dorm. Apparently, it was an on-court issue of some kind, but I wasn't sure. He just kept yelling at me. I was always sensitive about that, perhaps a little too sensitive. I finally yelled back at him and it turned into a shouting match. He kicked me out of practice and told me not to come back until I got my act together. I was so angry I told him I was leaving and not coming back. And I was serious.

I quickly took a shower, went over to my dorm room and began packing. But I started thinking, Oh, my gosh! What did you just do? I hoped somebody would come talk to me.

Finally, when practice was over, one of the basketball managers came and told me to think about what I was doing. I told him I just didn't like anybody yelling at me, especially in front of everybody.

"After you calm down, why don't you go talk it over with the coach, just you and him," he said.

I continued packing and said, "I'll see."

After he left, I took a deep breath and realized he was right.

The next morning, I went in to see coach Ireland. We had a very good conversation. After the meeting, he never yelled at me again.

Every now and then coach Ireland would take me with him when he scouted local high school ballplayers. He took me to a game at St. Rita's one night, and I was impressed with the Reuther brothers, John and Joe. At 6-foot-8½, Joe Reuther was the tallest player in the Catholic League. John was a tad shorter at 6-foot-7 but had a turn-around-jumper that was nearly unstoppable.

At the end of the game, won by St. Rita, Ireland asked me what I thought about Jack Egan, a 5-9 guard.

Egan?

"He's all right," I said. "But I'm more impressed with the two Reuther boys and their height."

I didn't know coach Ireland had already looked at other big men from Nashville, Tennessee, as well as Floyd Bosley from Chicago's Crane Tech High School. Ireland arranged for another player to scrimmage at Loyola, 6-foot-9 Rich Rochelle, a star center for Evanston High. After the scrimmage coach Ireland asked me about Rochelle. "He's all right," I replied. "But he has great potential."

One summer day before my sophomore year, I went over to Alumni Gym to scrimmage with some Loyola players and new recruits. I saw Egan, Rochelle and Bosley, but not the Reuther brothers.

During the full-court scrimmage, I could tell right away Bosley could really jump and Rochelle had some defensive talent. After the scrimmage, coach Ireland called me to his office and told me I had a big surprise coming.

"I'll see you in my office tomorrow," he said.

My immediate thought: the Reuther brothers! Later, I found out the Reuthers had decided to attend the University of Louisville, where they backed up my assessment. Both started for the Cardinals. John Reuther, who passed away in 2016, is one of the leading scorers and rebounders in Louisville history and is in the Louisville Athletics Hall of Fame.

When I went to coach Ireland's office the morning after the scrimmage, he introduced me to 6-foot-6 Vic Rouse and 6-foot-7 Les Hunter, both from Nashville, Tennessee. Vic and Les made immediate impressions on me. It's difficult to put into words, but I only had to look at them to know they were good players.

One of the best high school basketball teams in the country during the late 1950s, led by Ronnie Lawson, Vic Rouse, and Les Hunter.
They captured 3 consecutive National Negro High School Championships.
Photo courtesy Pearl High Sports.

When we finished our first scrimmage together, I realized I was wrong: They weren't good. They were *very* good. With Rouse and Hunter, plus Miller, Egan, Rochelle, Bosley and a pair of additional Catholic high school recruits Chuck Wood and Jim Reardon – the scrimmage rose to another level. The 6-foot-3 Chuck Wood was an all-state selection from a great team at St. Catherine's High School in Racine, Wisconsin. The 6-foot-4 Jim Reardon starred for Chicago's St. Leo's.

I had just come off an *easy* 23-points-per-game freshman season. Now, going against them, I could feel the pressure to compete. Getting off my shot was more difficult, especially driving to the basket. It was tough, much tougher, and I loved every minute of it. I knew these guys wouldn't just "show up" for the games, they would come at you in every practice, every scrimmage. I knew they would make me a better player and I thought I could return the favor.

So, I knew we had something special. National championship? No, I wasn't going there just yet. But, Loyola had finished with losing records the previous two seasons (11-13 and 10-12). I knew the losing days were over.

Coach Ireland knew, too. After that first scrimmage, as I passed his office, he looked out at me with a big smile on his face. I smiled back just as big.

Chuck Wood (top row, second from right), one of the best athletes to come out of Wisconsin in the late 50s - finished runner-up in a national Catholic High School Tournament Championship to John Thompson, former Georgetown Coach, right below him in the picture.

One day after practice a guy I knew from Clinton came to the gym to see me. He made small talk and praised me for the year I was having, and we talked about the good times in high school. Then he got down to business.

"Jerry, I'm here to give you a chance to make some good money," he said. "We want Loyola to win their games but you just cut back your scoring a little bit and make a few turnovers here and there. Mind you, we want you to win the game, but just keep the score under the point spread."

He saw the quizzical look on my face and tried to explain.

"You know, if Loyola is picked to win the game by 12, win by eight. No harm done and you will take home some big bucks".

"I am in no way interested," I said. "No!"

"Jerry, they are doing it all over the country, believe me."

"No!"

"Okay, but if you have any questions or change your mind call me at the hotel. I'm taking a flight out tomorrow."

It was the same proposition I had received while living in the projects. I didn't do it then, why would I do it now while everything is starting to go well for me? Plus, I knew now it meant breaking the rules. I didn't know the guy that well, anyway. I also noticed that the two guys who approached me were white, so I thought of it as white crime, gambling at high stakes.

I always thank God for giving me the insight to do the right thing on serious issues such as that. The second offer was much easier to refuse than the first one. I understood the complete picture better. And a few months later, a point-shaving scandal was uncovered in college basketball. I ran to tell coach Ireland how happy I was that when I was approached, I said no. He said, "You were contacted and didn't tell me?" I said I didn't think it was that important since I had turned him down. In Harlem or the Bronx, we did not snitch on one another. But coach Ireland was angry. "Something like this," he said, "you always let me know, you understand!?"

He then rushed off to his office. He told me later he called the NCAA and they let him know I was all right.

Over the next couple of days, the names came out, led by Jack Molinas, a former professional player who ran an organized point-shaving operation. I was shocked at all the guys from New York and Chicago who were involved in the scandal. One was from Clinton, a guy from a well-to-do family. The ones I knew were nice guys who I thought were smarter than that, but they fell to the temptation of quick cash. The messenger who came to see me was right, a lot of people were doing it.

What shook me up was that they were kicking guys out of college, sending them home and making them appear in court. I thought if that was me, my mother probably would have gone into a deep depression. My whole family would have been negatively affected, as would my friends, my former teachers and men such as Walter November, Nick Kladis and Howie Garfinkel. It would have stained the good reputations of all the schools I had attended as well as my teammates and coaches at Loyola. And nothing I had been able to accomplish to that point would have taken place.

For years, I wondered what would have happened if I had agreed to participate in the point-shaving and approached Wayne Davis. Would I have gotten caught? Would he have turned me in? The answer is yes. Many years later, a friend of mine, Delano Bryant, a union leader and close friend of former Indianapolis Mayor Bill Hudnut, introduced me to the next Regional Director of the Federal Bureau of Investigation (FBI), who would be stationed in Indianapolis. His name was Wayne Davis - yes, the same Wayne Davis I was supposed to contact about shaving points. My questions were finally answered.

The new recruits would have to wait a year to become eligible to play varsity ball, but I was really looking forward to doing so my sophomore season. When we started to scrimmage, I was full of confidence and vigor. After I learned the plays, I was ready to go.

After we won our first five games against weak opponents, a couple of the veteran players came up to me and said, "Now is the time we start losing."

I couldn't believe it.

"Are you kidding me?" I said. "Do you really believe that?"

They told me to wait and see. I looked around and saw seniors Clarence Red and Jim Mini, junior Allen Ray and fellow sophomore Herm Hagan. Sure, that talented group of freshmen gave us all we could handle in the scrimmages, but we weren't that bad.

Yes, we lost our next game, but that was no disgrace. Ohio State was the top-ranked team in the country and the defending NCAA national champion. It was led by future pros Jerry Lucas, John Havlicek, Larry Siegfried and Mel Nowell and a future coach of note, Bob Knight.

We went on to get big wins over Marquette, Western Michigan, Wisconsin, Baldwin-Wallace and Detroit. The win over Detroit was the most impressive. We pressed – full court and three-quarter court – against the bigger, taller Titans the entire game. Led by Dave DeBusschere – who finished with a game-high 35 points – they went up by 12 points midway through the second period, but the fast pace finally caught up with them. We came back to win, 83-82. Despite fouling out with a little over a minute to go, I led our scoring with 25 points. Mike Gavin, a junior guard, was next with 19 and hit two free throws to ice it with 28 seconds left.

Our next game was against St. John's in New York City. Coach Ireland gave me a chance to go home to see my family the day of the game. I was on my home turf, but the game was to be played at Fordham University's gym in the Bronx. I got lost trying to find the arena and arrived just before the opening tip, with very little time to spare. Coach Ireland didn't say anything, but I knew he was angry. I led all scorers with 24 points, but we lost by that amount, 98-74.

As the regular season drew to a close, we were one victory away from receiving an NCAA tournament bid. It was plain and simple: beat Xavier in the season finale at Chicago Stadium, and we get an at-large tournament bid. But if Xavier wins, it goes to the tournament.

Loyola (Chicago) 1960-61 team. We just missed the tournament bid 15-8.
Courtesy Loyola Sports Department.

Xavier shot great and led by as many as 22 points in the second half. Our press finally started to wear them down, but we couldn't catch up. Xavier won, 94-85, to advance to the tournament.

We ended the season with a 15-8 record. Everybody was overjoyed. Everybody except me. I was truly disappointed. I had never lost that many games in one year. Eventually, I tried to focus on the positives. I ended up with 520 points, a 22.6 season scoring average, and 150 free throws. All three were school records and I received the team's Most Valuable Player award.

Coach Ireland was disappointed about failing to qualify for the NCAA tournament, but that didn't last long. He had a lot to look forward to with such a powerful freshman team on the way to join the returning varsity players. It seemed as if something special was on the horizon.

Jim Mini holding his Free Throw Award. Clarence Red, the Team Rebound Leader, and I was voted MVP.
Courtesy Loyola Sports Department.

Coach Ireland let everyone know how excited he was before the 1961-62 season began, bragging to the media about the talent he had accumulated. He turned out to be right. We went 23-4, ranked tenth in the final Associated Press regular season poll and finished third in the National Invitation Tournament (NIT) at Madison Square Garden.

We had received invitations to both post-season tournaments but coach Ireland opted for the NIT over the NCAA because it meant our players would miss fewer classes. It also was a favor to our New York City natives, Ron Miller and me.

LOYOLA UNIVERSITY OF CHICAGO, 1961-62

We reached a ranking of 10th in the nation with our 23-4 record. Front row left Jerry Verway, Dennis McQuade, Jack Egan, Mike Gavin and Ed Schilling; Second row left Chuck Petraca, Jim Reardon, Les Hunter, Rich Rochelle, Floyd Bosley, Vic Rouse, John Crnokrak, Coach George Ireland, Top row left Allen Ray, Chuck Wood, Jerry Harkness and Ron Miller. *Courtesy Loyola Sports.*

My junior season included wins over Duquesne, Detroit, St. John's, Wisconsin, Michigan and Indiana. The victory over St. John's at Chicago Stadium was special because most of the Redmen players were my New York heroes: Willie Hall, Leroy Ellis, Donnie Burks, Ivan Kovac and Kevin Loughery. I was able to break the school's single-season scoring record and again be named Most Valuable Player.

We also were in the headlines off the court because of our trip to New Orleans to play a local college, also named Loyola. As soon as our plane touched down, the black players were separated from the white players. We rode in separate cabs. We couldn't stay at the hotel with the white players, so we stayed with local black families instead. A couple of us stayed with the family of Clarence Red, who was from New Orleans. Three stayed with a minister friend of Vic Rouse's family.

The segregated arrangements were disturbing at first, but the experience turned out well for the black players. The black community in New Orleans treated us like kings. We had all we wanted to eat, outstanding music and beautiful young ladies for dancing and conversation. We had an absolutely fabulous time. I always laugh today when I tell Jack Egan how much fun we had while he and the other white players were hung up in a hotel.

Needless to say, we were fired up for the game, which ironically was played on the same date Jackie Robinson was elected into the Baseball Hall of Fame. We were ahead by 30 at halftime and coasted to a 96-73 victory. I led all scorers with 29 points while Vic Rouse and Les Hunter each scored 24.

The small number of black fans in attendance made their presence felt. They sat together and cheered loudly from start to finish. Loyola of New Orleans was a great host and we had no problems at the arena, and the game ended without incident. Afterward, Ireland complained about the segregated environment and said, "Under the circumstances, I don't think we should play here again."

Ireland continued to make headlines back in Chicago. He told reporters there the entire team was scheduled to stay together in New Orleans at Xavier University, a small, Catholic, predominantly black school. But, he said, he was informed upon our arrival in New Orleans that if blacks and whites stayed together the team would be arrested.

However, the dean of Xavier University refuted Ireland's claim, stating his school offered to house and feed the entire Loyola team and that Ireland had decided to seek separate accommodations. I can understand Ireland's resistance, given what he was told about the attitude of civic leaders in New Orleans about blacks and whites staying in the same dormitory.

My grades improved throughout my time at Loyola. I was actually going to the library to study – a novel concept, I know. But even there I wasn't shielded from racism. One day, I was checking out a book and, naturally, had to show my library card to the person at the checkout desk. A pair of varsity teammates, Mike Gavin and John Crnokrat, showed up. Gavin looked at my ID and said, "Wow, you sure are *black!*

I started for him and then remembered what my mom told me: Don't get into any trouble, like fighting. Don't do *anything* that might get you kicked out.

While "Crno" laughed, Gavin professed innocence, saying, "What did I do wrong?" I wanted to hurt him, but I walked away. When I got a chance, I looked at the picture on my student ID card and realized Gavin was right - at least from a photographic standpoint. The photographers for the school's identification cards did not adjust the lighting for black students. My photo was under-exposed and I was indeed extremely dark. Still, I think Gavin could've saved his observation for a more private setting.

I did not have any racial problems with students in class or the dormitory. I have no doubt there were racists at Loyola, like anywhere else, but they stayed away from us or kept their opinions to themselves. I also discovered racial stereotypes weren't confined to African Americans. One night in the dorm a bunch of students were watching "The Untouchables" on television, a highly-fictionalized series inspired by the work of Eliot Ness in bringing down Al Capone and the Chicago Mafia. A student of Italian descent walked over and turned off the television. I realized right away he did not like the way Italians were being depicted in the series. For me, it was a minor epiphany: Hey, black folks aren't the only ones who are sometimes stereotyped in a negative way.

I also vividly recall that nobody got up to turn on the television again until "The Untouchables" was over.

Social life for the black players on campus was non-existent. One Friday night, while we lounged at the dorm, as bored as could be, somebody mentioned that there was a party at Mundelein College, an all-girls school connected to Loyola's campus.

Almost everybody said, "Let's go!"

About eight of us showed up at the door. You could see the girls – all white – were startled but they were cordial and let us in. We walked over to a table with punch and finger sandwiches and started to strike up conversations – with each other. We must have arrived a little early; no other guys were there yet. So, we started talking to some of the girls. We could tell they were nervous; I'm sure most had not socialized with black males. As I chatted to one of the guys, I could see Earl Johnson, a good freshman ball player from Cleveland, really laying it on a scared-to-death young lady. I walked over and told Johnson to cool it. He told me she was "starting to come around."

I looked at the girl and I could see tears in her eyes. She was shivering as she excused herself.

Starting to come around? We didn't stay much longer, because it was obvious we weren't welcome. Henry White, a track star and self-styled comedian, yelled out, "Drip-mouth Johnson scared all of them with his smile."

We all laughed and went back to the dorm to watch television – but not "The Untouchables."

The next morning, all the black basketball players got word that coach Ireland wanted us in his office at 11 a.m. I think we all had an idea what this meeting was about. We settled in his small office, some standing, others sitting around him. He told us he just got a visit from a nun from Mundelein College. "I see you wore out your welcome," he said.

I told him we weren't welcome from the moment we got there.

Ireland went on to say that in the next 20 or 25 years this would change, there would be more integration. But now was not the time. The nun told coach Ireland the girls were afraid of us.

Ron Beals, a transfer player, spoke up. "I don't care. If they are fine, I go for them," he said.

"Yeah, you are ready but they are not," the coach explained. "Let's think it out before we jump to a decision."

To deal with that dilemma, the black players arranged a small get-together in the lounge area of the dorm the following week. We invited the few black girls who attended Loyola and the black nurses from Providence Hospital. Herm Hagan, who was from Parker High in Chicago, knew some girls, too. We got a record player and some of the girls brought records. We had soft drinks and sandwiches from the cafeteria.

To make a long story short, we had a blast! We danced and socialized all night to popular steps like the Watusi and Kill That Roach (which called for us to stomp as if we were killing roaches). We also danced the Madison and the Monkey while the always-agile Les Hunter, one of the best dancers in our group, led us in the Mashed Potato. Chubby Checker had just re-released the Twist. For the second time in three years, Checker topped the charts and, the dance of the same name became a national craze. We gladly contributed to the renewed Twist mania. We even got some of the white students from the all-boys dorm to dance. That dorm rocked! The only complaints came from a few of the dorm residents who were trying to study that night.

I learned a lesson during my junior year, a lesson which played a part in our future success.

It happened in a game against the Blue Streaks of John Carroll University, a small Catholic school in Cleveland. We had beaten them easily the previous season, 108-47, and that was without Hunter, Rouse, Egan and Miller. I certainly didn't expect any problem with them this time.

When the game started, they broke our vaunted full-court press with crisp passes and showed no signs of panic, as many of our opponents did. They also ran a patient, deliberate offense, effectively getting the ball into their best shooters' hands. Right away I realized their scouting reports had us down pat. They knew what each of us would do, especially on defense.

I must have been easy to scout. I kept doing the same thing I had learned in practice but they anticipated it and put us in a position which left Vic Rouse trying to guard two players, one low and another in the corner. It was hard to hear with John Carroll's home crowd screaming throughout the game, but that didn't stop Vic from yelling at me, "Make the adjustment! Get your man!"

I yelled back at Vic, not exactly an indication of team harmony. Coach Ireland saw the conflict and took out Rouse, our best rebounder and one of our top defenders. But Vic was right. I wasn't playing smart defense. As a result, the John Carroll players could anticipate what I was going to do almost every time. The game was tied 13 times in the first half and we trailed at half-time, 34-31.

I made a few adjustments on defense, which helped some. We went on a 12-4 run to start the second half and took a five-point lead. But we still couldn't shake John Carroll. The game remained tight, deadlocked another half-dozen times in the second half. With 10 minutes left, the score was tied at 49.

Rouse came back in the game late in the second half but John Carroll still hung tough. With less than a minute to play, Carroll's Ray Maria – who led all scorers with 28 points – sank a pair of free throws to put his team on top, 66-65. With 35 seconds left, I tipped in a missed shot to put us back on top by one. With four seconds remaining, the Blue Streaks got the ball to forward Don Gacey for a 15-foot jump shot. As Gacey went up, Rouse went right with him. I could see Vic's hand go up high, high enough to force Gacey to arch his shot a little more than usual. The buzzer went off with the ball in mid-air. Gacey's shot appeared on target. When the ball came down, it hit the inner right side of the rim, rolled around to the left side and popped out. The ninth-ranked Loyola Ramblers survived, 67-66.

I then saw something I had never seen before and, to this day, haven't seen again. Although Loyola won, the John Carroll fans rushed onto the court cheering, and hoisted Carroll players up on their shoulders. As we walked off, heads down, I had to look up to the scoreboard to make sure we had, in fact, won the game. I also made brief eye contact with Vic and quickly put my head down again.

The scoreboard notwithstanding, there were a number of winners that night. First and foremost, the John Carroll players deserved the adulation from their fans. They were extremely well-prepared and, with far less talent, put up a fierce battle.

But I won, too. I learned to quit playing like a robot. If we were to realize our full potential, we had to play smarter. I had to play smarter. That experience also made me realize how vital Vic Rouse was to our success. Hard-nosed? Without a doubt. But Vic was level-headed at the same time, a rare combination. We never had a disagreement on the court again. As a matter of fact, no one on our team ever did.

About a week before the start of the 1961-62 basketball season, we heard about a house party in Evanston. Five Loyola athletes – all African Americans – decided to go. A friend dropped us off. It was wonderful, at first. The food was excellent and the black girls were attractive and friendly. The guys, however, were lukewarm at best.

I had been in this situation before, but on the other side. When guys from the outside came to socialize in the Patterson projects, they were not welcomed by me or my friends, especially if the girls showed an interest. Upon hearing some harsh remarks from the Evanston guys, we knew it was time to go.

We didn't have transportation, so we decided to walk about six blocks to the Howard Street station for the "L," Chicago's elevated train. A casual walk quickly turned into a mad dash. As soon as we got outside, we heard somebody yell, "Where are you guys going? The party is just getting started."

It didn't matter that we were in the process of leaving. They wanted to guarantee we never return – *ever*. There were about 15 of them so we were badly outnumbered.

Henry White, a Loyola track star, said, "I'll see you guys" and bolted. The rest of `us followed immediately, although Vic Rouse got off to a slow start. They gave chase, yelling while hurling bottles at us. A couple of bottles crashed next to me, which motivated me to pick up my pace. Once again, I was thankful for my track and cross-country background as I was able to put the voices in the distance.

When I reached the "L" station, Henry White was there, already fully recovered. Then came Earl Johnson, Les Hunter, Allen Ray, Herm Hagan and, finally, Vic Rouse. Our next concern was the "L" – would it be on time?

Fortunately, we saw no signs of the Evanston gang and the train arrived about five minutes later. Once aboard the "L," Vic told us how a couple of the gang members grabbed his jacket while another waved a knife. We then noticed Vic's back was bleeding, near his right shoulder. We cut off the bleeding as best we could with someone's undershirt.

After we got back to our dormitory, one of the dorm managers did what he could to treat Vic's wound, but he told us it was worse than we thought. Vic wound up in the emergency room at the hospital. The injury wasn't terribly serious, but Vic's shoulder blade was heavily bandaged and he couldn't move his arm for a short period.

We spent some anxious moments waiting for Vic to return from the emergency room. But, like most college jocks, once we found out he was okay we made light of the incident. Vic just smiled when we teased him for being so slow.

Coach Ireland was livid when he found out about the incident, and for once his ire wasn't directed toward us.

"Nobody treats my players like that!" he shouted.

Coach Ireland made a few phone calls and, within a week, the police tracked down the culprits. I'm told that once pressed in the interrogation, the gang members turned on one another. They eventually went to court. In all, 13 were convicted and fined. The guy that stabbed Vic also received a 30-day jail term.

I would never want to measure someone's toughness with a stabbing, but if you had to pick someone who had the grit and determination to come back quickly from such a setback, it would be Walter Victor Rouse. After breaking his nose during a second-half fight against North Dakota early in the 1961-62 season, Vic was expected to miss two or three games. He sat out one. A minor inconvenience like a broken nose wasn't about to keep him on the bench.

Chapter 9

THE 1962-63 SEASON

Our best team was not the one that captured the NCAA tournament in 1963. It was the team that won another tournament a couple of months earlier, a holiday tourney in Oklahoma City. We beat Arkansas, Memphis State and Wyoming to extend our season-opening win streak to 10 games. What was more important to me is that for the first time in Division one history five African American players were in the game for Loyola when Jack Egan was kicked out of the game by an official and replaced by Pablo Robertson. We didn't realize history had been made until years later.

LOYOLA UNIVERSITY—Back row, left to right: Earl Johnson, Billy Smith, Vic Rouse, Leslie Hunter, Jim Reardon, Rich Rochelle. Middle row: Paul Krucker, (assistant coach), Ron Miller, Chuck Wood, Captain Jerry Harkness. Head Coach and Athletic Director George Ireland. Front row: Manager John Gabcik, Dan Connaughton, Jack Egan, Pablo Robertson, Trainer Dennis McKenna.

Oklahoma City Tournament winners.

We lost our two best reserves from that group in early February after grades came out: sixth man Billy Smith and seventh man Paul "Pablo" Robertson. Smitty, a 6-5 sophomore center, was a great inside scorer and rebounder. He played well in that Oklahoma City tournament and then played a crucial role in our next game, a come-from-behind win over Indiana in Bloomington, Indiana, when he came off the bench to score 14 points, 12 in the second half. Pablo, a 5-9 guard, was a floor leader and uncommonly mature for a sophomore. He gave Egan and Miller breaks, and sometimes provided a boost with his flashy play.

We were a much better team with them than without them. But we had to carry on.

We had six regular-season games remaining after losing Robertson and Smith. Although Coach Ireland publicly downplayed the losses, the local papers immediately speculated as to how the reduction in depth might affect us.

Note that any reference I make concerning media reports is information I picked up much later, from reviewing old clippings in my scrapbook or reading past articles people sent to me. At the time, when I was playing, I was largely unaware of what the press had to say. I think that was true of my teammates, too. We were more concerned about preparing ourselves to be the best we could be rather than what outsiders thought of us.

However, looking back, I can understand why the roster depletion (which included the transfer of sophomore Earl Johnson) might have fueled speculation. Over those last six games we lost twice, needed overtime to win one game and eked out a four-point victory in another. And our scoring average dropped by 17 points.

Lack of depth was a factor, but not the only one. We played some good teams down the stretch and in some hostile environments. The starters were sorry to lose their teammates and friends, but we never talked about how it affected our performance on the court.

Our first game following the loss of Robertson and Smith – and our first game in ten days – was against Marquette, part of another doubleheader at Chicago Stadium. The Warriors, as they were called then, were a natural rival for Loyola because the two Jesuit universities are located only 85 miles apart, about a 90-minute drive when traffic conditions are favorable. It was the kind of rivalry in which rankings, records and past results didn't mean much. The fact we had defeated Marquette, 87-68, earlier in the season at their place was no guarantee of an easy victory. And we didn't get one.

Although Marquette would eventually finish the season with a 20-9 record (including two wins in the NIT), it was not enjoying the kind of season it had hoped for. Its roster was depleted much like ours because of an injury to starting forward Bob Hornak, who had missed a month of the season, including the previous game with us. With Hornak back, a game against the undefeated, second-ranked Ramblers of Loyola provided the Warriors a great opportunity.

The game was tight most of the way and was tied at halftime and at the end of regulation. Marquette frequently beat us at our own game: the fast break. I was fortunate to score twice in the last minute of overtime, including a steal and layup that gave us a 92-90 victory. I finished with 26 points but Ron Miller had 28 to lead all scorers.

"This was the closest brush with defeat for Loyola," Richard Dozer of the Chicago Tribune wrote, "a game in which its ineligibility losses and a 10-day layoff undoubtedly reduced the team's effectiveness."

While it's true that three of our starters played much of the game in foul trouble and coach Ireland hardly used our reserves, I prefer to think Marquette's talent and tenacity was a greater factor in the closeness of the game.

Four days later, the still-undefeated Ramblers hit the road to face an unranked but dangerous Bowling Green team. The Falcons spent much of the previous season in the Top Ten but, like Marquette, had under-performed in the first half of the 1962-63 season. They split their first 12 games and lost three-straight in early January.

By the time we faced them, though, the Falcons were on a roll. We caught them in the middle of an 11-game winning streak to close out the regular season. Yes, Bowling Green wanted us badly, and so did their fans. Their gym was packed and the noise was deafening. I could barely hear the entire game. But I won't pin our fate that night on "home court advantage" or "lack of depth." They flat-out beat us. The Falcons jumped out to a 9-0 lead and never trailed. The final score was 92-75, snapping our winning streak at 21 games. Komives scored 32 points while Thurmond added 24 (18 in the second half). I don't know if any team could've beaten Bowling Green that night. Ironically, top-ranked Cincinnati lost that same night, 65-64, to Wichita State.

Two days later, on Feb. 18, Loyola was one of eight independent schools to accept an at-large bid to the NCAA tournament. The remainder of the 25-team field would be filled as the conference races played out. On the very morning that Loyola officials accepted the NCAA invitation, the *Tribune's* Dozer speculated, "The loss of reserve personnel, however, might convince Loyola's athletic board that an adventure into the National Invitational tournament in New York would be wiser than a trip to the meet."

I wasn't aware of Dozer's conjecture at the time and, while I wasn't privy to discussions with Coach Ireland and the athletic board I doubt rejection of an NCAA bid was ever seriously considered. Yes, Loyola had opted for the NIT the previous year – and for valid reasons, I think – but not two years in a row. Especially with a very real chance of winning the more prestigious tournament. I also think coach Ireland wanted to make a statement with our racially mixed team of four black stars and wanted to do so on the biggest stage.

Our lack of depth never entered our minds as we prepared for the tournament but looking back it's obvious that if one of our starters had fouled out, we would have been in trouble. Fortunately, that never happened.

We celebrated our NCAA tournament acceptance with a 70-47 win at St. John's that night. Nine days later we whipped Ohio University at home, 114-94. Wedged in between that pair of easy wins was a nail-biter at Houston, a game I consider pivotal to our team's development.

Chapter 10
HOUSTON (A TEAM BUILDER)

On Feb. 23, 1963, we were greeted by a loud chorus of boos when introduced at Jeppesen Gymnasium for our game against the Houston Cougars. Though near the University of Houston, Jeppesen was located off-campus. That made it easier for people who weren't students or alums to attend the game and made for a most hostile atmosphere.

We encountered a large, boisterous crowd as we ran through the tunnel and up the ramp toward the court. Fans were screaming insults at us, such as "You think you're tough because you're ranked? We are going to beat your a____!" We had grown accustomed to similar reactions on the road. After all, we were 22-1 and ranked third in the nation. The Houston fans, however, seemed a little more agitated than the norm.

I usually didn't check to see if there were black players on the opposing team, but this time I did. Houston was like most teams we faced: all white. I also noticed very few police officers were on hand.

The game was a little on the physical side but nothing out of the ordinary. The score remained close through the first half, but I felt we had control even though we were up by only two points at halftime. As we walked off the court, the crowd was even more hostile. They moved in closer to us and threw popcorn and ice. Some of our players were sprayed by a cup of soda pop. I was relieved to reach the protection of the dressing room.

As coach Ireland went over strategy for the second half, my attention drifted. After he finished, I went over to Ron Miller and asked, "Do you think these people are going to come out of the stands after us?" Ron simply shrugged his shoulders. Finally, coach Ireland got us together for our usual end-of-halftime ritual. We put our hands together in unison and yelled, "Go, Ramblers!"

As we exited the locker room, I was worried. The fans were louder, angrier, shouting threats such as, "Come on out here, you black monkeys,you niggers! We got something for you!" And, "Our team is red hot! Your team is all black." They even called our white players albinos.

71

It felt like these crazy fools were right on top of us and ready to attack. They threw popcorn, ice and water onto the court. I was still in distress as we stepped onto the court to begin the second half. With so few police officers available to maintain order, there was nothing to prevent fans from coming after us on the court.

I felt the pressure and was worried through most of the second half. Although I finished with a team-best 17 points, I probably hurt the team more than I helped. Les Hunter and Vic Rouse, the Nashville natives who were more accustomed to this kind of hostility, helped us pull out a 62-58 victory. It was our lowest point total of the season, well below our nation-leading 93.5 points-per-game.

We still had to get back to our locker rooms, though. The screaming and name-calling as we ran through the tunnel was still loud, but not as harsh.

In the locker room I told Vic, "All it would've taken was one fool to charge us and the rest would have followed."

"Let's just shower and get out of here," he said.

I don't remember any post-game comments from coach Ireland. I do remember how all of us rushed to get out of there and onto the bus. Once we got back to the hotel, a few of us met in the lobby to go out to eat. We went to a restaurant two or three blocks away. I felt leery as we entered, but we just sat down at a table and waited for someone to come by with menus.

A man came over and said, "You can order here, but you will have to take it out. You cannot eat here."

"You got to be kidding me," I said.

I was still upset about our treatment at the game. Hearing this just made it worse. Ron Miller said, "You heard the guy. Let's get out of here."

From my childhood trips to Virginia, I remembered the "For White" and "For Colored" signs above bathroom doors, water fountains and on restaurant walls. But there were no warning signs here in Houston.

We got up and left. There were some muttered complaints, mostly by me. I did feel some satisfaction that the man's racism had cost him a good sale, but it still hurt.

As a team with five black players and four black starters, we encountered occasional hostility, in varying degrees. The trip to Houston had felt the worst, however. Maybe it was the worst because we were blindsided. Maybe we thought, as many people did, that racial divides were relegated to the

Southeast ... states such Alabama, Mississippi and Georgia. We didn't expect it in Houston. A later examination of that city's racial history told me we should have been more prepared.

Houston's coach, Guy Lewis, apologized to us after the game. Ironically, he didn't waste much time after that recruiting black ballplayers. Elvin Hayes and Don Chaney were the first at Houston. They were joined by Melvin Bell and Theodis Lee on Final Four teams in 1967 and '68 and on the team that stopped UCLA's 47-game winning streak in that momentous regular-season game at the Astrodome in January of '68. Hakeem Olajawon, Clyde "The Glide" Drexler and Otis Birdsong were among the great African American players who led Houston to basketball prominence from the late 1960s through the early 1980s.

Some 50 years after our Houston experience, our Loyola team was inducted into the College Basketball Hall of Fame. Among the Hall of famers was Elvin Hayes, a Louisiana native who enrolled at Houston only a couple years after our incident there. In three seasons at Houston, Hayes averaged 31 points and 17 rebounds per game. The "Big E" followed up his incredible college career with an impressive pro career, becoming a 12-time NBA All-Star.

In his acceptance speech, Hayes made a point of thanking the Loyola Ramblers for what we did to further the integration of college basketball.

We met eighth-ranked Wichita State in our regular season finale on March 2 at Chicago Stadium. The Shockers were led by future NBA players Dave Stallworth and Nate Bowman and had upset top-ranked Cincinnati, so we knew we had our work cut out for us.

The game was close from start to finish. Like Houston, the Shockers were able to slow down our offense and we trailed at halftime, 30-28. Our dearth of reserves did factor into this loss, I think. We could have prevailed because of our tendency to wear down the opposition, but Les Hunter and Vic Rouse fouled out - Les with 6:20 remaining in the game, Vic about 30 seconds later. We missed Smitty in that game, someone to give Vic or Les a breather when they got into foul trouble.

To their credit, the Shockers converted free throws down the stretch, cashing in four times on one-and-one opportunities. Stallworth, who finished with 28 points, gave Wichita State the lead for good on a three-point play after a foul call on me, a foul referred to as "questionable" by the Chicago Tribune. Wichita State won, 73-72, so we headed to the NCAA tournament with a 24-2 record.

Chapter 11
HISTORY IN THE MAKING

Our first game in the NCAA tournament was against an all-white Tennessee Tech team that had a 16-7 record but showed improvement late in the season. Their coach had a game plan he truly thought would beat us. They were going to slow the game to a crawl and then play a zone defense to try to take advantage of their superior height.

Before the game, Egan ran into John Adams, a reserve center for Tennessee Tech who had played with Jack on his St. Rita High School team in Chicago. Jack seized the opportunity to joke with him in the hallway before the game to put him on edge. Adams, knowing Egan's personality, didn't want to be bothered. Jack being Jack, followed his former teammate into their locker room and continue talking to him. Egan could tell that Adams was a little tight and asked if everything was all right. After not receiving an answer, Egan smiled and told Adams, "Just take a deep breath, it's going to be over really quick." Egan made sure to speak loudly enough for Adams' teammates to hear and walked out the room.

We not only had a psychological advantage, we had homecourt advantage. The game was played at Northwestern, just a half-hour from our campus. More importantly, we had more talent and chemistry, which led to a historic outcome.

Let me explain, 1963 was a key year in the Civil Rights movement. African Americans across the nation were expanding their fight for equality. They weren't just talking; they were taking action in a non-violent way.

For example, Howard University and Morgan State students got together to battle the segregation of a Northwood theatre in Washington D.C. The students protested and were put in jail, but after a week of protests, city officials agreed to end segregation of the theatre. All across the South, African Americans rose up against segregated public facilities and demanded better employment opportunities and a greater role in the political arena, such as through voter registration. Blacks were joined by whites in nonviolent activities such as sit-ins at segregated restaurants, sing-out rallies, marches, prayer vigils and picketing, all in a demand for equality.

In Chicago, black students and their parents marched in protest of overcrowded public schools. They weren't allowed to transfer to all-white schools that had room for them.

Learning more about those activities later, I understood why so many African Americans contacted me at Loyola. Some were friends wishing me well in the NCAA Tournament, others said simply, "You've got to win." We drew further motivation from the inspirational songs we heard on radio and television, such as "Precious Lord" and "We Shall Overcome."

We never discussed it, but when we took the court to play Tennessee Tech I could see it in our players' eyes. Each one was highly motivated and on top of his game. We jumped out to a 61-20 halftime lead and wound up hitting 56% of our field goal attempts in a 111-42 victory. The 69-point win remains the most lopsided in NCAA tournament history, and it reflected our balanced attack. Ron Miller led our scoring with 21 points. I had 19, Egan and Rouse had 18 each and Hunter chipped in with 17. It was one of the few games that season every team member played.

We definitely were motivated by the Civil Rights Movement. Incidentally, Adams, Egan's teammate in high school, only scored one point.

Excited and confident, we couldn't wait for our next game to be played four nights later. We had a dilemma, though. We only had nine players available for practice, which made it difficult to prepare because we didn't have a "second five" to emulate the opponent. That would have been impossible anyway in this case, because we didn't even know the identity of the next opponent.

All we knew was that it would be another all-white team from the South, specifically a representative from the Southeastern Conference, which, unlike us, received a bye in the opening round of the tournament. We were an independent team and therefore ineligible for a bye. Mississippi State, ranked in the nation's Top Ten, had won its final four regular season games, all on the road, to finish the season with a 12-2 conference record.

The Bulldogs closed out the regular season on March 2 with a hard-fought win at Mississippi (led by future Chicago Cub Don Kessinger) to earn sole possession of the SEC championship. Nearly two weeks later, however, we still didn't know if Mississippi State would be our next opponent.

The hang-up led to one of the most historic moments in college basketball.

It was uncertain if Mississippi State would accept the NCAA tournament bid it had earned by winning its conference championship. It seems inconceivable now, the idea of a team refusing to go to the tournament, but it had happened before. Mississippi State had already refused to participate in the tournament in 1959, '61 and '62 because of a university policy of not playing against teams with African American players. Not just us, the team with four black starters, but any team with even a single African American on its roster, whether in the regular season or a tournament.

In December of 1956, Mississippi State had played in a holiday invitational tournament in Evansville, Indiana. The Maroons (the MSU nickname at the time) advanced to the championship game of the tournament against Evansville College. Shortly before the championship game, however, it withdrew from the tournament because the host school had an African American player.

Ben Hilburn, Mississippi State's president at the time, said the order to withdraw came from Athletic Director C.R. Noble. Hilburn said there was no order from the state legislature to prevent State from playing against black players in games outside of Mississippi, but "we just want to play like we play here at home."

If Mississippi State had continued to follow that unwritten rule in March of 1963, we would have faced Georgia Tech, the SEC runner-up, in our second tournament game. However, Mississippi State's head basketball coach, James Harrison "Babe" McCarthy, previously quiet about the segregation rule, was quoted in a newspaper article saying that although he would follow the direction of his bosses, he felt "the majority of people in Mississippi would favor our playing integrated teams out of the state."

While waiting to find out who we would play – Mississippi State or Georgia Tech – we continued to work on our full-court and half-court press, even though the win over Tennessee Tech gave us confidence in our defensive pressure. We had been perfecting it for two years. We had to add an assistant coach when working on our half-court press and a freshman player when working full court.

When we got back to the dorm after practice, I picked up a letter I thought was fan mail. The first thing I saw, in big letters on the envelope, were the letters "KKK."

1962-63 S. E. C. CHAMPS

Members of Mississippi State's 1962-63 Southeastern Conference Championship basketball team:
Front Row, left to right - Coach Babe McCarthy, Doug Hutton, Stan Brinker, Captain Joe Dan Gold, Bobby
Shows, Leland Mitchell, W. D. (Red) Stroud, Assistant Coach Jerry Simmons.
Second Row - Manager Jimmy Wise, Don Posey, Larry Lee, Jackie Wofford, Howard Hemphill, Billy
Anderton, Aubrey Nichols, Freshman Coach J. D. Gammel. Missing from picture Richie Williams.

1962-63 Mississippi State Team. *Courtesy Mississippi State Sports Department.*

It shocked me; I didn't even read the contents right away. A minute or two later, I sat down in the dorm and started reading. "Hey nigger, you don't deserve playing against white folks. Stay home if you know what's good for you." It was signed, "KKK."

I had another hate mail postcard in my small batch of letters. This one called me a "tar baby" and said I should "stay with picking cotton."

I called coach Ireland and told him about the letters. He raced over to the dorm and collected all the mail. That's when I found out some of the other black players also had received hate mail. Ireland told the mail collector that if any suspicious mail came in to his black players to give him a call. He would come over and take a look at them.

Ireland said something like, "Don't worry about that white trash ... ignorant fools."

That was good advice ... to a point. Easy to say; difficult to do. I was still a little frightened because they obviously knew where I lived. I know coach received more hate mail, but we never saw any more of it. Later in life, I'm told Ireland gave the letters to his daughter, Judy. With all this going on – and not knowing who we were going to play in the tournament – I had the feeling things were starting to unravel around us.

Our team rode a bus to East Lansing, Michigan, the site of our next game on the Michigan State campus, still not knowing who we were going to play. When we got to our hotel rooms, we got the news that Mississippi State would break the color barrier. The Bulldogs would be our next opponent.

At that time, we didn't know anything about the trials and tribulations they had gone through to do so. The first inkling came when I went out to meet the Mississippi State captain, Joe Dan Gold, at midcourt before the game. I'll never forget all the camera flash bulbs that were popping as we shook hands. It startled me at first. Then I looked into Joe Dan's eyes. He wasn't smiling, but I could sense a friendliness. I felt he was glad to be here playing against us.

One of the referees cited last minute instructions, which I did not hear. I was in the moment with Joe Dan and the constant camera flashes. Then I started to realize this was more than a game. It was history in the making.

1966 I FRIENDLY PERSUASION was used by
Boston's Bill Russell in a plea to an apparently oblivious
Mendy Rudolph. I *Photograph by* WALTER IOOSS JR.

1963 I THOUGH VILIFIED for playing against blacks,
Joe Dan Gold's Mississippi State team took the court against
Jerry Harkness and Loyola. I *Photograph by* RICH CLARKSON

I was still in a slight daze as I jogged back toward our bench, thinking about what I had just experienced. Coach Ireland's voice grew louder and louder, however, as he went through final instructions about keeping the pressure on. When we went out for the jump ball, I was in full game mode.

We started slowly. The Bulldogs went up by six points and slowed the tempo of the game nearly to a crawl. They were tough and they were physical, but nothing dirty. If there was any racial animosity – by either side – it didn't show on the court.

We learned from previous games, such as the John Carroll contest, to maintain our composure, keep the pressure on, and to play smart and together. Once we got the lead and gained control of the tempo, we were all right. We won, 61-51. I led the scoring with 20 points.

They were much better than I expected them to be - fundamentally sound, talented and well-coached. They proved that in the regional's consolation game, when they defeated the same Bowling Green team that had defeated us pretty handily earlier in the season.

Harkness scores after a slow start.

Coach
Babe McCarthy

I appreciated the Mississippi State team even more after I found out what they had gone through just to play us in the NCAA tournament. Dean Colvard, the relatively new president of the University and coach McCarthy – expecting a backlash – put a strategy in place which nearly resembled a CIA covert operation. After the regular season finale, the victory against Ole Miss, Colvard announced to the press that he was sending his team for the first time to the NCAA tournament. That put pressure on the school's board of trustees, who called a special meeting. There was a proposal to prevent the team from playing in the tournament, but it was voted down, 8-3. The board went on to give Colvard a 9-3 vote of confidence, after a motion requesting Colvard's resignation was denied. More than two hundred students went to Colvard's house to voice their approval.

The board's decision inspired a group of segregationists led by Mississippi Governor Ross Barnett to obtain an injunction that ordered President Colvard and Coach McCarthy "from allowing any Mississippi State athlete to compete in any athletic contest against members of the Negro race." Colvard then called a meeting with McCarthy and Athletic Director Wade Walker, among others, to devise a plan to avoid getting served with the injunction.

Babe meets the press.

McCarthy and Walker immediately traveled to Tennessee, while Colvard went to Birmingham, Alabama, where he had a speaking engagement already scheduled. The Mississippi State players, hearing all kinds of rumors, waited anxiously in their dorm rooms for their next move. It didn't take long. The team trainer and some of the non-starters and scrubs were told to head to the airport to see if a sheriff was there to serve the injunction. It was directed at Colvard, Walker and McCarthy rather than the players, however. After the "all clear" sign was given to the starters and other officials, they rushed to the airport and flew to Nashville, Tennessee. There, they met coach McCarthy and Walker. The sheriff went to Colvard's house to serve the injunction, but he was long gone.

As it turned out, just about everybody was in support of the team going to the tournament except a relatively small group of powerful and influential politicians. More than half of the Mississippi State students signed a petition supporting the Bulldogs' entry in the tournament. The Mississippi State players, in a poll by a local newspaper, unanimously expressed their desire to play.

The book *"Champions for Change,"* by Kyle Veazey reported that a reporter named Robert Fulton from the Jackson, Mississippi *Clarion-Ledger* published comments from some of the players regarding playing against African Americans:

Leland Mitchell: *"I don't see anything morally wrong with playing against Negroes, Indians, Russians or any other race or nationality. Most of the boys have already competed against them in High School or in hometown sandlot games."*

Red Stroud: *"Competing in the NCAA would give us a chance to win a National Championship for Mississippi State. The memory of getting that chance would be a lot better than having to live with the memory of not getting the opportunity."*

Captain Joe Dan Gold: *"I think our going to the NCAA would help the school's publicity. It would make the whole state of Mississippi look less prejudiced and it would make it appear the state is trying to work out a solution to its problem of competing on the same level for national championship and prestige."*

Bobby Shows: *"When I was young we used to choose up and play against Negroes and it didn't affect us then. In my opinion, playing against them and playing to beat them up there won't be a form of integration because we are playing against them and playing to beat them. I think the majority of people want us to go. In a democracy, the majority is supposed to rule."*

Stan Brinker: *"I would like to go because I came from Illinois and I've played against Negroes before. After you get out on the floor they are just ballplayers and part of another team you are trying to beat."*

Billy Anderton: *"It is the main desire of every ball player to go to the NCAA. That is the big thing. If you're not planning to go to the tournament what are you playing for? I don't believe our going will bring on integration."*

Two years later, in 1965, Dr. Richard Holmes became the first African American to attend Mississippi State University. No incidents took place.

I'll forever be grateful to the Mississippi State players and school officials for making such a daring and historic move. A large crowd of supporters met them at the airport after they returned to Mississippi, proving that the majority of people there supported their decision.

Sports is more powerful than we think. Our victory over Mississippi State advanced us to the tournament's Elite Eight, where we were to play Illinois, the Big Ten representative. I always played well against Big Ten schools for some reason and I had perhaps my best game of the tournament against the Illini, scoring 33 points in a 79-64 victory. We outrebounded them, 57-35, with Rouse pulling down 19 rebounds, and dominated them in just about every other category, too. I enjoyed playing against my high school rival, Bill Burwell, again. He had played for Boys High in Brooklyn when I played for DeWitt Clinton.

Nick Kladis, a former Loyola basketball standout, told me I was going to have an outstanding game against Illinois. He had been such a great supporter of mine that some people thought he gave me gifts and money, but I'm happy to say it never occurred. He did give me a summer job in his grocery store, but we were just good friends.

Harkness and
Nick Kladis.

The night of our victory over Illinois, Ron Miller and I were reliving the game in our hotel room when somebody knocked on the door. It was coach Ireland.

"Wood and Egan broke up some bikes and we just got them out of jail," he said.

Ron and I were stunned.

"They have to be dealt with," coach Ireland said. "That Wood can never be trusted to do right. Egan follows him all the time. Let me know what you come up with."

"Coach, how do you know they broke the bikes?" I asked. "Did some-one see them? The police let them go, didn't they?"

"We'll talk tomorrow," he said. "See ya."

After he left, I asked Ron what he thought. We had just reached the Final Four and had already earlier lost Smitty, Pablo and Johnson. We would lose a starter and our new sixth man and be down to seven players.

Ron smiled and said, "Tough decision." The next day, Coach Ireland went over to Chuck and Jack and said, "You're lucky. The players said we don't have enough evidence."

Chapter 12

THE FINAL FOUR
Duke, March 22, 1963

The win over Illinois earned us a trip to the national semi-finals at Louisville's Freedom Hall. The building was only seven years old at the time and located within the Kentucky State Fairgrounds, a few miles south of downtown Louisville. With a capacity of more than 19,000, it was one of the largest basketball venues in the country and quickly became a favorite site for the tournament's final games. It already had hosted the Final Four in 1958, '59 and '62 and would do so again in 1967 and '69.

> *(Note: the term "Final Four" was not yet in vogue but has been retroactively applied to all of the semi-finals in the NCAA tournament.)*

This also was several years before the NCAA began seeding the tournament. The pollsters did a good job of predicting the tournament finalists, though. The final Associated Press poll ranked Cincinnati, Duke and Loyola 1-2-3 and all were still alive. The exception was Oregon State. The Beavers (22-7) came in with more losses than the rest of the semi-finalists combined, but they had upset fourth-ranked Arizona State, 83-65, in the final of the West Regional. Oregon State drew two-time defending national champion Cincinnati in the semi-final round. We got second-ranked Duke.

Coached by Vic Bubas, Duke matched our 26-2 record and brought a 20-game winning streak into the tournament. It was undefeated in Atlantic Coast Conference games and swept the ACC post-season tournament. (At the time, the ACC was one of the few conferences to stage a post-season tournament.)

The Blue Devils were led by Jeff Mullins, a 6-4 forward and future NBA All-Star, and Art Heyman, the consensus NCAA Player of the Year. Heyman, a 6-5 forward, averaged 25 points over his three-year varsity career. I knew

Art from New York. He was from Oceanside, in Nassau County, and we met up a few times on the city playgrounds.

That year's Final Four was well represented on the All-America teams. A couple of weeks earlier, Heyman and I were selected first-team All-America by the Associated Press, as was Cincinnati's Ron Bonham. Cincinnati's Tom Thacker was a second-team selection and the Bearcats' Tony Yates made the third team. Another Cincinnati player, George Wilson, was an honorable mention All-American, as were Mullins and Oregon State's Mel Counts and Terry Baker. Sports trivia buffs will point out that Terry Baker is the only person to win college football's Heisman Trophy and play in the Final Four.

The individual recognition was nice, but far down on my list of priorities. I prefer to be introduced as "captain of an NCAA championship team" rather than "a former first-team All American." I was disappointed, though, that my teammates did not receive more individual recognition.

Les Hunter was probably the most underrated player on our team. He was an excellent passer, a superb *blind* passer. He loved to hit you with a pass without looking. His outlet passing off of rebounds was outstanding. The layups and easy shots that complete fast breaks tend to get most of the attention, but the outlet pass after a rebound set them up.

Les would go through prolonged stretches in which he didn't even touch the ball, especially when our opponents had weak guards. Egan and Miller had so much anticipation and speed that they often stole the ball and got easy layups before Les could get downcourt. One time, when we had one of our big halftime leads, Les said, "Say, just let me touch the ball once in a while, fellas. I'll give it back to you."

He looked as if he was going to cry. We had smirks on our faces, but we made sure he got the ball as much as possible in the second half. We wanted to keep Les happy. He was our center, the nucleus of our team.

Les touched the ball plenty in our Final Four victory over Duke. He scored 29 points and pulled down 18 rebounds while I chipped in with 20 points and 11 rebounds. Duke cut our 13-point halftime lead to three points, 74-71, with 4:19 left to play, but got no closer. We outscored the Blue Devils 20-4 in the final four minutes to run away with a 94-75 victory. One of the highlights in that run was my breakaway basket, a play that began when Les blocked Art Heyman's shot.

Les would go on to make the all-tournament team, but he should've been named the tourney's Most Valuable Player. He finished runner-up to Heyman for that honor. Heyman scored 29 points against us and scored 25 points in the consolation game when Duke beat Oregon State for third place, but his team didn't even play in the championship game.

LOYOLA OF CHICAGO   1963 NATIONAL BASKETBALL CHAMPIONS

Rich Rochelle
Les Hunter
Vic Rouse
Chuck Wood
John Egan
Capt. Jerry Harkness
Coach George Ireland

Jim Reardon
Dan Connaughton
Ron Miller
Mgr. John Gabcik
Asst. Mgr. Fred Kuehl
Trainer Dennis McKenna
Asst. Coach Jerry Lyne

Loyola (Chicago) 1963 - Record 29-2.

Championship Game -
this is how it happened.

Chapter 13

THE NCAA CHAMPIONSHIP
CINCINATTI, MARCH 23, 1963
Defense Matches Offense

I was really worried about our opponent in the championship game, the top-ranked and two-time defending national champion Bearcats of Cincinnati.

We had seen them play at the Chicago Stadium in late January, a doubleheader that featured the top three teams in the country at the time: 1) Cincinnati, 2) Loyola and 3) Illinois. The Bearcats and Illini squared off in the second game. We had the easier assignment in the first game against Santa Clara. The twin bill attracted a *suspected* record crowd. It was reported at 20,687 for the 19,100-seat arena, a little off the official stadium record. However, several ushers told local papers they believed 4,000 to 5,000 were standing, pushing the *actual* attendance closer to 25,000, the largest crowd ever to attend a basketball event in the building.

Cincinatti Bear Cats - 2 time NCAA Champs.
Courtesy of Cincinnati Athletic Department.

We beat Santa Clara, 92-72, out-rebounding the bigger Bronchos, 64-41. Les Hunter had another big night with 27 points and 18 rebounds. I added 23 points and had to move to the backcourt as Miller played sparingly. Billy Smith – one of the players we were about to lose – scored 18 points and pulled down 14 rebounds.

Watching Cincinnati and Illinois play in the second game, I could see the Bearcats' talent, especially on defense. I pictured Tom Thacker guarding me. Like me, he was an agile, 6'2½" small forward, not a bit of fat on his body. He wasn't fast-fast, but awfully quick. He was a great defender, but not much of a scoring threat from the perimeter. We were similar in many ways.

I had played with George Wilson in a neighborhood game while he was still at Chicago's Marshall High School and I was a freshman at Loyola. We stayed on the floor the entire time because we won every game. Four years later, I could barely recognize him. He might have felt the same about me. We both had come a long way from those pickup games. I don't remember if we even said a word to each other back then, even between games. After nearly two-and-a-half hours on the court, we quietly went our separate ways. Who knew we'd meet again three years later at Louisville's Freedom Hall for the national championship?

The night before the championship game, we all were in our hotel rooms on the same floor. It was late at night, but no one could sleep. Some of us were gathered in Vic Rouse's room when we began saying to one another, "We must win!" Rochelle, Les, Vic and I then started yelling, "We gotta win!" Bobbing our heads backward and forward, we repeated the phrase over and over, lifting our arms in the air and dropping them back to our sides. "We must win!!!"

Hearing the commotion, Miller came in, looked at us, shook his head and left. Rouse, whose father was a preacher, started moaning, groaning and preaching. Then Les, Rochelle and I grabbed pillows and began hitting each other, still yelling, "We must win!" with Vic preaching and Les Moaning. It was quite a scene. We kept this up, along with other shenanigans, for about two hours.

We didn't go to bed until three or four o'clock in the morning. After an early breakfast – which seemed even earlier to us – we rushed over for our shoot-around at Freedom Hall. We were dead tired. This is, by no means, an excuse for our slow start against Cincinnati. It just shows how silly and immature young men like us can be, trying to psyche ourselves up for a game we knew was going to be very close - just trying to get an edge.

Our bus arrived at Freedom Hall about two hours before tipoff. There were people at the entrance asking for autographs and calling out our names. That was different, but neat. I looked at some of the faces and recognized a few from Loyola. I waved and shook hands with a few people as I entered the arena. Assistant coach Jerry Lyons was the first person I saw in the locker room. He patted me on my back and then clapped his hands. With his high-pitched voice, he said, "This is it! We are one win away from winning it all! It's going to be beautiful!"

Coach Ireland was the next person I saw. He didn't say anything, He just kept staring at you until you looked into his face, then he would smile. We all took our time getting taped up and tried to keep the conversation lighthearted with small talk and jokes. A couple of players got dressed early and went out to shoot around, but most of us stayed in the room.

More than 19,000 fans came to witness the clash between the best defensive team in the country, Cincinnati, and the best offensive team, Loyola. I looked into the stands and could tell the crowd was fired up. This was the first year the NCAA championship was televised nationally but our fans back in Chicago couldn't watch us live. The game was tape-delayed on WGN-TV until the finish of a Chicago Blackhawks hockey game. It's difficult to believe today that the NCAA and the television networks didn't realize the gold mine they had in such a game.

Years later, the tournament was branded "March Madness." It was expanded to 64 teams and beyond, quite different than the 25-team field in 1963. Needless to say, it raked in millions of dollars. The television coverage exploded, too; even the announcement of the tournament field - "Selection Sunday" – was turned into a live national broadcast, with remote shots of exuberant teams reacting to their selection.

The tournament of 1963 was nothing like today. But the championship meant as much to us as any team that's played in it since.

As I watched, the Cincinnati Bearcats warm up, I knew this was going to be a very difficult game to win. Just like Bowling Green with its 6-foot-11 center, Nate Thurmond, Cincinnati had a major defensive presence in the middle in George Wilson. I also watched Tom Thacker, one of the best, if not *the* best, defensive player in college basketball. Tony Yates made very few mental errors as the floor leader. Southpaw Larry Shingleton could shoot and played his part in their team defensive setup. Their scorer, Ron Bonham, was a great shooter but also a complete player.

Throughout college I was never more worried about an opponent than Cincinnati - not because they were the top-ranked team in the country or because they had won the previous two national championships, but because they matched up so well with us.

Early in the game, my worries were validated. I tried to surprise Thacker by going to my right instead of left, as most southpaws do, to try to catch him off-guard. The next thing I knew, the ball went out of bounds. He had come over my right shoulder and slapped the ball out of my hand without fouling me. I couldn't believe it; nobody had ever done that to me before. I was trying to gain a mental edge on him, but it turned out to be a setback that affected me almost the entire game. I had been apprehensive about him, and this confirmed my fears.

I began searching for ways to get out of my funk as the game progressed. I would drive to the middle and finally get by Thacker, but Wilson would be waiting. I tried to pass the ball inside to Hunter, but Thacker or Bonham would pick him up and I wound up forcing bad shots.

The Bearcats, meanwhile, were patient on offense, working the ball around until they got a good shot, no matter how long it took. That worked most of the time. Wilson controlled the boards while Yates and Shingleton controlled the tempo, Thacker led the defense and Bonham handled most of the offense. They dominated us, and we were fortunate to be down only eight points at halftime.

Coach Ireland was calm and confident in the locker room, telling us we couldn't have played any worse and yet were still close. "Once we start playing our game we're going to be all right," he said.

I bought in, thinking Yeah! Coach is right!"

At the start of the second half I did something I don't think I had ever done before: I talked to my opponent. I dared Yates to shoot. I backed off from him when he was a foot or so behind the foul line and told him he couldn't shoot. He smiled, shot and hit nothing but net. He smiled at me again as he ran back on defense and said, "Thanks." I couldn't believe it. According to the scouting reports, Yates didn't look for his shot often. He mostly ran the offense. From there, Bonham hit three straight jumpers to lead a surge that put Cincinnati up by 15 points just six minutes into the second half.

We called time out, and I can remember praying to myself, "Dear Lord, if we have to lose, please let it be close." I thought of my mother, father and friends in the projects seeing me play so bad. Ireland remained positive with us. As the huddle broke, I said, "Let's go," under my breath. Somebody else yelled, "We still got time!"

Above:
Key time out.

Right:
Hit my first basket with about 5 minutes to go in the game.

We fought back a little and pulled to within seven points at 48-41. Then with about five minutes to go I made my first basket. We began pressing them and I stole the ball and scored again. With about a minute to go we were down by only three points and I had the ball. I drove to the basket on a fast break and put up a layup. It felt good, but it bounced off the rim. But Les tipped it in.

We were trailing by a point with 17 seconds left when I fouled Shingleton while trying to steal the ball. He had a one-and-one opportunity at the free throw line. As he prepared to shoot I said a silent prayer: "God have him miss one, just one." I didn't want to be too greedy ... I felt God already had helped us get this close. But, I knew if Shingleton hit both free throws and gave Cincinnati a three-point lead, the game likely was over. The three-point shot didn't exist then, and it would have been virtually impossible to catch up.

Shingleton, a lefthander like me, hit his first free throw to give his team a 54-52 lead. But his second attempt hit the front rim and fell off. Les secured the rebound and passed to Ron, who took a couple of dribbles and passed to me on the left. I took a dribble and quickly put up a shot. I wasn't feeling a thing. I just let it go. If I had shot an air ball, I wouldn't have been surprised. But the ball went in ... nothing but net! The game was going to overtime.

I've always believed a higher source helped me make that basket. The feeling I had was almost other-worldly. It was as if I was in a trance. Only as we all started back toward the bench did I become aware of all the cheering and yelling – from the crowd and from my teammates.

Coach Ireland shouted out numerous instructions in the huddle, but most are a blur today. I do remember he said, "Okay, we have the momentum. Let's jump on them right away. Don't let up now. You worked too hard to get back in it. You deserve it! *Don't let up!*"

When we lined up for the jump ball, that's exactly what I told myself: *Don't let up!* With Vic Rouse jumping, I thought of running to our basket, hoping to get a quick outlet pass. It worked exactly that way. Vic tipped the ball to Les, who passed it to me. I dribbled and laid it up on the right side of the basket. But I wanted to be sure, so I shot it with my left hand.

We traded baskets for a while. George Wilson scored from in close for the Bearcats. Ronnie Miller answered with a big bucket for us, a 20-footer that gave us a 58-56 lead. I watched him take the shot and thought of those thousands of shots I saw him take in practice. Shingleton then caught up to a long pass and laid it in to tie the score at 58.

With a little less than two minutes to go, we decided to hold for the last shot. We were moving the ball very well – ironically, just like the Bearcats had done – until Jack Egan got tied up with Shingleton with 1:21 remaining. This was before the alternate possession rule, so every tie-up resulted in a jump ball. Jack controlled the tip and we continued our stall. With nine seconds to go, it was time to make a move to the basket. I got the ball and drove to the left baseline. I stopped and went up for a short jumper, but Ron Bonham tipped the ball while I was going up. I still had control but just didn't feel comfortable. I saw Les out of the corner of my eye, wide open near the foul line left of the basket because George Wilson had left him to get in position for a rebound. I passed the ball to Les, who went up for the shot as Wilson rushed back towards him. The shot bounced off the rim, but right into the

hands of a soaring Vic Rouse. Without coming down, Vic put the ball back up and *in*! The buzzer went off and Loyola had won, 60-58. On the radio, our announcer Red Rush was screaming, "We won! We won! We Won the ball game!" Freedom Hall exploded. Our players, coaches and trainers mobbed ... yelling, screaming, hugging and holding each other. Then came the cheerleaders to join in the celebration.

Rouse hits the winning shot.

I said to myself, "Thank You, Lord. Oh my gosh! Yes, to the Jesuit society!"

When things calmed down and we lined up for the awards, I remember going out to receive the championship trophy. It was so heavy I called for help from Vic and Les. It was appropriate - they had carried me throughout that championship game.

It was especially noteworthy for Vic Rouse.

Vic, who wore braces on his legs throughout most of his childhood.

Vic, who wore weights on his ankles during practice to strengthen his legs.

Vic, who was stabbed in the shoulder during his junior year.

Vic, who had his nose broken at least twice in college.

Vic fought through it all, as he did in the title game, leading us to the shocking comeback. I think any of our guys would have been deserving to hit the game-winner, but nobody earned it more than him. Vic truly deserved to hit the biggest shot in Loyola basketball history, or, as the *Chicago Tribune* called it, "The Shot Heard 'Round the Basketball World."

The post-game interviews after our victory seemed overwhelming, and really were for the time. The amount of media coverage was minuscule compared to what today's college athlete must withstand, but today's coverage of the tournament is more organized - sometimes overly-controlled in the opinion of some reporters. I was getting more accustomed to the media exposure, through repetition if nothing else. That explosion of flash bulbs before the Mississippi State game was eye-opening, literally and figuratively.

The attention was exciting, even welcomed for the most part. But, it delayed the most enjoyable

Forward Vic Rouse would not be stopped by injuries.

part of the victory: sharing it with teammates, friends and fans. It was so enjoyable just to talk with my teammates before we caught the bus back to the hotel. I can't remember any of the specifics, it was just championship chatter. It's the *feeling* of the moment I recall.

Back at the hotel, coach Ireland called us to his room. He directed us to the view from his window. I don't ever remember him as excited as he was at that moment, as he pointed at the scene below. Down on the street, hundreds of fans were screaming and rocking a car and a small bus. Confetti filled the air. Fans were hugging one another. A school from Illinois had never won a major college basketball title and they were making up for it.

When we found our seats aboard the plane for our return flight, I put on a pair of sunglasses. I was sitting by myself, stylin', feeling on top of the world. But one of the trainers walked over and informed me that coach wanted me to take off the glasses. I paused for a second and thought, *you know, he's right. What am I doing? What was I thinking? That's not me.*

Or was it? Regardless, the shades came off.

The starting five front row left Vic Rouse, Les Hunter, and Asst. Coach Jerry Lyons, back row Jack Egan, Capt. Jerry Harkness, Coach George Ireland and Ron Miller
Courtesy Sports Illustrated.

As our plane descended toward the runway, I was surprised to see fans waving at us. About 2,000 people were there to greet us. When the airplane door opened, we were met with a wall of noise. I was the first off, the plane, carrying the enormous championship trophy. The fans began screaming, "We're Loyola! We're No. 1!" We were led to an area where Mayor Richard Daley and other dignitaries were standing behind a huge sign that read, "Welcome Home Champs." They congratulated us and posed for pictures with us. I can't tell you everyone I posed with or shook hands with. I had never experienced anything like that before and haven't since. It was breathtaking.

But it wasn't over. Next came a motorcade to the Loyola campus for a pep rally. More introductions. More cheers. More adulation. During the next couple of months, we attended several victory ceremonies, all of them wonderful. But there was nothing like the "juice" from those early homecoming celebrations.

Of all the awards and remembrances, we have received over the years, one stands above all else: having our numbers retired by the university, immediately after the season. I had been voted the team's Most Valuable Player as a sophomore and junior, but the entire starting lineup received the honor my senior season – to my delight.

Mayor Daley greets us at the O'Hare Airport in Chicago, Illinois.

Our game with Cincinnati was a landmark event on many fronts.

One that I'm very proud of today, and was essentially unaware of at the time, is that it was the first Division I NCAA championship basketball game in which the combined starting lineups for both teams were predominantly African American. For the second straight year, a team with four black starters took the opening tip. Cincinnati had done it the previous year with Paul Hogue, Tom Thacker, George Wilson and Tony Yates. Only Hogue graduated, so the Bearcats returned three black starters to face Loyola with its African American starting quartet of Les Hunter, Ron Miller, Vic Rouse and Jerry Harkness.

Seven black players started a national championship game in an era when many Southern schools allowed no African Americans on their teams and when many Northern colleges imposed an unwritten quota on how many could play or start. That means more to me because of the challenges and prejudices I experienced, in and out of sports, while growing up in Harlem. To be a part of it, even a small part, in 1963 – a year so pivotal in our nation's Civil Rights Movement – is very special to me.

Chapter 14
COLLEGE ALL-STAR GAMES

After the NCAA tournament, I received word that I was selected to play in both college all-star games for seniors throughout the country.

The first game was in Lexington, Kentucky, a benefit for the Naismith Basketball Hall of Fame. I played on the East team, which also included Duke's Art Heyman, the national Player of the Year, Cincinnati's Tom Thacker, Bowling Green's Nate Thurmond, Indiana's Jimmy Rayl and Mississippi State's Red Stroud. We pulled away down the stretch to win, 77-70. I remember making a pass behind my back to Heyman who laid it up and was fouled. Heyman led our team with 14 points, including 12 in the second half, and was named the game's MVP. I was next with 13 points.

1963 College All-Stars - I'm in the middle holding the ball.

The more memorable game for me was the second one a week later at Kansas City's Municipal Auditorium, with proceeds going to the Shrine Crippled Children's Hospital. Thurmond, Thacker, Heyman, Stroud and Rayl were all on the East team again but I was put on the West team, mostly with guys I had never heard of before the game in Lexington.

I wondered how that had happened, and also wondered how much I would play. Due to final exams, I arrived late in Kansas City and missed the team's two practice sessions. During our pre-game chalk session, our coach told us to just have fun. "We don't need to have any plays," he said. "Just play together, pick and roll, fast break when you can and enjoy yourselves."

I didn't start. I didn't like that but understood. As the game was about to begin I realized I had played against all of the East starters and wondered if the West group of less-heralded players had a chance. During his final instructions, our coach had a unique calmness about him. He smiled and said, "You all are the best in college basketball. Just enjoy playing together as a team."

We went out and did just that, taking a lead we never relinquished. We led 48-32 at halftime and held off a late East rally to win, 82-79. I finally got my chance eight minutes into the game. I decided to make the most of it. I finished with 14 points and several assists. I was voted the game's Most Valuable Player, although it easily could have gone to a number of my teammates, such as Ken Charlton of Colorado, who led us with 15 points. Nolen Ellison of Kansas, Tony Cerkvenik of Arizona and Gary Marriott of Kansas State also scored 14 points.

Afterward, our coach was smiling as he came over and asked me, "Did you enjoy yourself?"

"Oh, yes!"

The coach's name: John Wooden. Coach Wooden and I had a good relationship from then on. When he came back to his hometown of Martinsville, Indiana, whether to visit the grave of his wife, Nellie, to see friends, or for a speaking engagement, I would always try to meet with him, especially for an interview during my career as an Indianapolis sportscaster with WTHR Channel 13 and later, WTLC Radio.

UCLA Coach John Wooden

We spoke about many basketball issues but I was most impressed with his love for his wife. He was a wonderful man and always made me feel special. He obviously made his players and other associates feel the same way, given the love they all showed for him after his coaching career ended. I realize coach Wooden led UCLA to its first Final Four in 1962, but as far as I'm concerned coaching that underdog West team to victory in the 1963 College All-Star Game was the beginning of his dynasty. John Wooden was a winner in all aspects of his life.

Thanks to my Loyola team, I was a unanimous All-American in 1963.

Chapter 15

GRADUATION

My Mom and Aunt Clara flew in for Loyola's graduation ceremonies on June 11, 1963. Their arrival in Chicago also provided me with the opportunity to introduce them to my wife-to-be, Judy Carroll, who they liked very much.

I knew Mom was really proud of me when I walked across the Arie Crown Theater stage at Chicago's famed McCormick Place to get my Sociology degree. I was one of 860 Loyola students who received a degree that day. I'll bet Mom was only vaguely aware of my 859 fellow graduates.

Mom

Aunt Clara

I also was thinking of her with every step I took. I even forgot to flip my tassel. It was so good to be with her and my aunt at such a happy time in my life. I couldn't help but think, *This could have easily gone another way ... and probably would have gone another way, if not for my mother.*

I hope this memoir will serve as thanks to every person who was responsible for my appearance on that stage, but I would be remiss if I didn't express my sincere appreciation to Loyola University. Sure, the NCAA championship was tremendous. It changed my life, and I know most of you wouldn't be reading this had it not been for the title. But that college degree, and more importantly, what it took to achieve it, enhanced my life.

So, I have to thank Loyola University. Those nitpicking, demanding Jesuits wouldn't let me go through their school simply focused on basketball. They demanded I be the best student I could be, the best person I could be.

After the formal commencement ceremony, I tried to introduced Mom and Aunt Clara to everybody I knew, not only because they were my relatives but also because I thought they were so pretty. I was proud of them, too, for many reasons.

Soon after my mother and aunt left to go back to New York I got a call from a wealthy family in Winnetka, Illinois, wanting to know if I could stay with them at their home. Their son, Kenny, had watched our NCAA championship victory and was overwhelmed with joy. Kenny's reaction also a source of happiness for the parents.

You see, their son, who was about 16 years old, was having some nervous and mental problems. Kenny would go off on his own, walking around the house, talking to himself and twitching his hands. But during the game they noticed he had full control of himself and was really focused. The father was a psychiatrist and had tried everything to help him. The mother asked me if I could spend some time with Kenny during the summer months. They would pay me, give me my own room and the maid would see that I was well-fed and cared for.

I accepted the job and spent time with both of their sons, John and Kenny. John was fine, he was energetic and loquacious, but I also got along really well with Kenny. We played basketball together and talked. The family was somewhat happy with the results as Kenny was better when he was around me, but he still had problems. His parents were a little strange, but I liked them quite a bit. They worked hard for the betterment of both their sons. The mother would cry some times when we had our nightly discussion about Kenny.

Kenny was truly a good person. I checked on him from time to time after that summer, and even visited him in the hospital. The doctor and attendants were amazed at Kenny's improved behavior when we spent time together, but he continued to have problems throughout his life.

Chapter 16
KNICKED BY THE KNICKS

Following my graduation and summer with Kenny, I began what turned out to be a brief career with the New York Knickerbockers.

At the end of April, the Knicks had selected me with the ninth overall pick in the NBA draft. That would be a lottery pick today, but I was the first pick of the second round because there were only nine teams in the NBA at the time and only eight participated in the first round because the Cincinnati Royals forfeited their selection by taking Tom Thacker as a "territorial pick" prior to the draft.

The territorial concept was discontinued after the 1965 season, but prior to that an NBA team could select a college player from any territory within a 50-mile radius of its home arena. It had to forfeit its first-round pick to do so, however. From 1949 through 1965, 23 players were selected as territorial picks, including 12 future Hall of Famers.

Right away, I started getting calls from the Knicks' coach, Eddie Donovan. He told me how happy the organization was to get me so early in the draft. The club planned to play a fast-breaking style, and I would fit right into their plans. Donovan then offered me a contract for $12,000. To put it in perspective, $12,000 in 1963 would be the equivalent of about $96,000 in 2017 - not a bad living wage, but pocket change for an NBA player today.

I refused that offer, asking for a $15,000 no-cut contract. Donovan said he couldn't do that, but he would get back with me. A couple of days later he offered me a $10,000 salary and a $2,000 signing bonus, which I also refused.

I was initially excited when I heard from the Harlem Globetrotters. They only offered me $8,000 but also, as they said, "A chance to see the world." I didn't look at that as a positive. I thought about all those games the Globetrotters had to play, many of them on consecutive days. I knew that would be too tough on my body. There was no need to negotiate a salary, I turned them down right away.

I also heard from the Akron Goodyears of the National Industrial League. They offered a good-paying executive job with the company while maintaining my amateur status in basketball. That would have allowed me to try out for the Olympic team the following year, and I was excited about that.

The Knicks called again, however, and invited me to meet them in their offices at Madison Square Garden. After being back home and around my friends, I weakened. I kept saying to myself, *Wouldn't it be nice to be home and help my Knicks get out of mediocrity?* I loved watching the Knicks while growing up in Harlem. Although they never won an NBA championship during my childhood, they were very competitive. They made the playoffs ten straight seasons and even reached the NBA Finals three straight years (1951-1953). Harry Gallatin, Nat "Sweetwater" Clifton and Dick McGuire all became Hall of Famers and Ken Sears, a two-time All Star, was another personal favorite.

I didn't follow the Knicks or pro ball much while at Loyola, so when they drafted me I wasn't fully aware they were in the midst of the worst stretch in franchise history, with four straight last-place finishes from 1960-63.

Still, the hometown atmosphere got to me, and on June 15, 1963 I signed a contract for $10,000 and a $2,000 signing bonus, caving on my previous "no-cut" demand.

After moving my family to New York, I got an apartment in the Dunbar, where I grew up. On September 10, I reported to the Knicks' training camp at the New York Military Academy in Conwell, N.Y. I could tell right away I wasn't in shape. I hadn't worked out and couldn't get into a groove, probably because of the time I spent with Kenny and his family.

It didn't help that I had to move to the guard position after playing forward in college. The guys I guarded were now just as fast as me, and I didn't have the shooting range to play guard. It was my fault for not being more prepared.

The Knicks already had two guards who were untouchable, Richie Guerin and Tom Gola, both seven-year veterans of the NBA. Gola's scoring average had been in double figures in each of his previous seasons and Guerin was the Knicks' top returning scorer, averaging 21.5 points the previous season. Art Heyman, who played both guard and forward, had been the No. 1 overall pick in the draft and also was guaranteed a spot.

Two less-heralded guards, Al Butler and Donnie Butcher, were entering their third seasons in the league and also outplayed me from the very beginning.

I played in the first five regular season games and scored 29 points. Coach Donovan then called me at home and gave me the bad news: I had been cut to make room for 6-foot-9 forward Tom Hoover, who addressed the team's need for more size.

My mom took it even harder than me. It was a low point in my life. Players were just beginning to hire agents at that time, but I had no one to negotiate for me. Many people connected with Loyola were sorry they didn't get someone to help me. But most things have a way of turning out for the best.

Chapter 17
A NEW LIFE

It was time for me to get a job and support my family.

My contract was not guaranteed, so the only money I had was what was left from my $2,000 signing bonus. A few weeks after the Knicks released me I played one game with the Trenton Colonials of the Eastern Professional Basketball League (EPBL), for which I was paid $200. That was actually more than the Knicks had paid me per game, even if you included my signing bonus - $12,000 over 80 games equals $150.00 per game. But, with only 28 games on the EPBL schedule, it hardly qualified as a full-time gig.

I also got a call from the Harlem Globetrotters to play with a team of college All Stars against the Globetrotters at Chicago Stadium. The Trotters paid me $300 plus expenses, which included a round-trip plane ticket. I had no choice but to accept. The Globetrotters agreed to make sure I wasn't on the floor when they performed all their antics. I received an outstanding ovation from the Chicago fans when I was introduced, something I really needed at that stage of my life.

I played well but, as expected, we lost to the Globetrotters, which pushed their "winning streak" to 525 games. The Trotters performed their usual comedic routines, which the crowd of 13,732 loved. At times, though, we played serious basketball and it was a relatively close game, 81-76. I scored 24 points to lead the All-Stars and former Michigan co-captain Bob Cantrell added 23. But the play of a pal of mine from New York, Connie Hawkins, put the Globetrotters over the top. Connie scored 28 points to lead all scorers and – Globetrotter shenanigans aside – it was obvious he was the most talented player on the court.

The return to Chicago and the chance to play against Connie again was fun and provided a needed payday. Basketball, however, wasn't paying the bills, certainly not all of them. I had my degree from Loyola but I needed a real job, and quickly... I went to a job interview at IBM and was called back, but no luck. With my bank account dwindling to just a few dollars, I nearly was at the point of asking relatives for help. I know they would've chipped in, but that would have been extremely embarrassing. Here I was, the All-American and first in my family to graduate from college – a great source of pride for the family – needing financial help?

Just in the nick of time, I got a call from The Quaker Oats Company, whose local district office was nearby in Elizabeth, New Jersey. I went for an interview and they hired me on the spot. I later learned Quaker Oats had sent word from its corporate headquarters in Chicago that I was to be their first black store sales merchandiser, which involved calling on retail grocery stores within the New York area. My starting pay was $375 per month, so it was a struggle to make ends meet at first. Our family, however, benefited from the perk of eating a lot of the company's products for free: oatmeal, grits, Aunt Jemima Pancakes, puffed wheat, puffed rice cereal, Captain Crunch and corn bread. Thank heavens we never had to eat Ken-L Ration dog food. All of the Quaker employees treated me well. I rarely felt like the only black on the sales team.

I got a nice raise and promotion a year later when we were transferred to Chicago, where I was to call on the big upscale grocery stores on the north side of the city. The logical thing, obviously, was to live in that area. I began looking for an apartment but kept getting turned away although "For Sale" signs and newspaper ads indicated they were available. Some of the apartments were close to Loyola. Finally, after a number of days searching, my family and I got a chance to see a nice apartment on Winona Avenue, which was relatively close to Loyola. I made the down payment and was relieved to have that behind me.

The next day I went to meet with the apartment manager, Mr. Lazarus, to get the keys so we could start moving in. Before I could say anything, Mr. Lazarus said, "Mr. Harkness, I'm so sorry but my dad already rented out the apartment without my knowledge. I'm so sorry."

Right away I thought, *This is not right. I'm being discriminated against.*

I didn't say much. I just got back my deposit and left. As I walked to my car, I started thinking that I could almost see Loyola from there. I pictured people running down the nearby streets to celebrate our NCAA championship victory, screaming out open windows, cheering, jumping with joy. No, I thought, it can't be discrimination. I would be a minor celebrity in this area.

But how did they mess that up, the son not knowing what the father had done? Jeremy Lazarus had seemed so nice and willing to rent to me.

I was confused as I got into my car.

Later that day, upon returning to my in-law's house, I received a call from Channel 7, asking what had occurred regarding the apartment rental. I wondered how they knew about my experience. They asked if I would like to speak on camera. I asked them to call me back tomorrow. I thought then it must have been true; I was discriminated against. I called my new supervisor at Quaker Oats to get his thoughts about the television interview. He said if I wanted to do it, it was all right with him.

After careful consideration, I decided against it. I wanted to get on with my life. We found a nice place at 67th and Paxton, on the South Side. Later in life, when I got a little more involved in Civil Rights issues, I was disappointed I did not follow up with Channel 7.

There was another incident to which I wish I had responded differently. For a while, Coach Ireland put the NCAA championship trophy in the barbershop across from the Loyola campus where they didn't cut African Americans' hair. We had to go all the way to Evanston. I wanted to go into the barbershop and take the trophy out but lost my nerve. I only got my shoes shined and left. I wish I had been more assertive. I made up for it later in life.

I was treated well on my job with Quaker Oats, calling on predominantly white customers in my territory. Some store managers and customers recognized me. I learned my trade well, grouping my Quaker cereal products together and putting them in an advantageous position in the store based on customer traffic in the aisles. I still recall the new Aunt Jemima syrup of that time and the slogan, "Aunt Jemima, what took you so long?" I enjoyed putting up Quaker displays such as the new cereal, Captain Crunch, which has done well for the company.

The Civil Rights movement had an effect on Quaker Oats, though. For one, Aunt Jemima was looked upon as a stereotypical figure from the past. The company was having black women dress up like Aunt Jemima, cooking pancakes at cookouts and greeting customers at select stores, but when under pressure from Civil Rights groups it stopped the program. A lot of black women around the country lost their jobs and complained.

Sometimes you have to sacrifice to make progress. I liked the Quaker Oats company. I thought it was on top of its merchandise, bringing out new products at the right speed, with excellent advertising and marketing.

The company also improved the image of Aunt Jemima, which had been introduced in the 1940s. When I started at Quaker, she had a scarf on her head. That became a full bandanna, but little by little the company shrunk the bandanna to a band. Then it took off the band completely. They curled her hair, gave her earrings, and made up her face. It's the same Aunt Jemima you see today. "Aunt Jemima, what took you so long?"

After two years I was promoted to a position Quaker had planned for me from the beginning: Promotional Athletics Administrator. The company started promoting Physical Fitness on the parking lots of grocery stores, roping off an area where children could run and participate in sit-ups, push-ups, and pull-ups. I was invited to the larger events around the country. I would sign autographs and award certificates bearing the Quaker emblem to those who met the standard. All others would get a certificate of participation. I also gave speeches. Most of the time an article would appear in the local newspaper showing me running a fitness event with youngsters. I enjoyed doing them but was not that keen on the administrative activities of the job.

It was relatively easy to understand the plans Quaker Oats had for me from the beginning: learn the business from the sales side and then help set up the athletic physical fitness program. General Mills had hired Bob Richards, a two-time Olympic pole vault champion and an ordained minister, as a spokesman for Wheaties breakfast cereal. He also set up the Wheaties Sports Federation, which encouraged participation in Olympic sports.

Quaker, as usual, went a step further by putting on the fitness events in the parking lots of large grocery stores. It was still conservative, however. One time, a U.S. Olympic swimmer named Donna de Varona came to speak at a Quaker Oats meeting. She was attractive and charming – a two-time Olympic champion at age 17, a cover girl on a number of major national magazines. I was the Promotional Athletic Administrator, but no one introduced me to her. I always thought that was strange. Maybe it was because I was too far down the chain of command. Or, maybe it was because she was a white female. I did meet her a few years later at a Special Olympics event. She, as expected, was very nice, and we laughed about that situation.

THE NEWS-PALLADIUM, BENTON HARBOR, MICH.

Hassle
h Draft

h. Richardson, Baltimore Colts, and e. linebacker Charlie Thornhill, o Boston Patriots.

Larry Conjar, the plunging in Irish fullback, reportedly has ne been signed by the Cleveland Browns. Offensive tackle Paul it Seiler was a first round pick of ti the New York Jets. Defensive oa end Alan Page went to the gh Vikings as a second round ip choice.

on The remainder of the Notre h Dame picks include: offensive tackle Tom Regner, Houston vo Oilers; center George Goeddeck Denver Broncos; defensive end g. Tom Rhoads, Buffalo Bills; line- er backer Jim Lynch, Kansas City Chiefs; defensive tackle Pete o' Duranko, Denver Broncos, a defensive end Alan Sack, Los b. Angeles Rams.

so, Michigan State Coach Duffy m Daugherty said it was embarras-sing in one way to have four of in his players go in the top eight of the first round choices.

is, "Now the fans are asking me ek how come we only tied Notre it- Dame with all that talent," he ig- explained.

PENTATHLON PRIZES: Twin City Sailors star and former Loyola All-Ameri-can Jerry Harkness displays certificate of achievement and hand exerciser which every participating youngster will receive at physical fitness penthath-lon to be held May 27 at Filstrup field. Entry blanks for the event will soon be available at all twin cities area schools. (Staff photo)

★ ★ ★   ★ ★ ★

Local Pentathlon Could Set R

Harkness Lauds Cooperation
Of Area Organizations

The youth physical fitness pentathlon scheduled for May 27 at Filstrup field as a cli-max to Michigan Week could easily turn out to be the largest of its kind ever held in this country.

That's the opinion of Jerry Harkness, Twin City Sailors star and national coordinator for the program which is joint-ly sponsored by the Amateur Athletic Union and Quaker Oats.

"I've helped put on close to

Softball League
Seeking Teams

There are openings for four more teams in the Benton Har-bor recreation softball league, according to league president Ralph Robards.

Any one interested in joining the league should call Robards at WA 6-6828 after 7 p.m. No teams will be accepted after Wednesday.

The league, now composed of eight teams, will open play on May 15.

200 of these events all over the country and I'm sure from the cooperation we're getting that we'll have at least 1,000 con-testants," Harkness said at a press conference Monday after-noon.

"The largest number we've had participate in any previous pentathlon is 1,156 in Provi-dence, Rhode Island. It looks like we could easily top this figure here."

The pentathlon is open to all area young people aged 8-18. Contestants do not compete against each other, but against a set of standards set up by the AAU for boys and girls in each of six age groups. Participating in the pentathlon will give a youngster an idea how he stacks up against an average American youth in his age group.

Twin cities Michigan Week co-chairmen J. Robert Bonomo

and Robert E. Schmid echoed Harkness' enthusiasm for the event, which will begin at 9:35 with registration.

"I've just been overwhelmed

Fraser Speaker
At Bangor Fete

BANGOR — Albion College football coach Morley Fraser will be guest speaker Thursday evening at the Bangor high school all-sports banquet.

Sponsored by the Bangor Vik-ing Club, the banquet will be held at 6:30 p.m. in the ele-mentary school all-purpose room.

Tickets for the banquet are priced at $2.50 per person and may be purchased in advance at the high school or at the door Thursday night.

by the cooperation we've gotten from the local schools and oth-er organizations we've contact-ed," reported Bonomo. "We're making arrangements for every pupil in grades 1-6 in the public and parochial schools of Benton Harbor, St. Joseph and Lakeshore to get an entry blank and letter of explanation to take home to his parents. Blanks will also be available at the schools for interested junior and senior high students."

Each youngster who partici-pates in the free program will receive a certificate of achieve-ment or a certificate of appre-ciation, plus a free gift. He will also be eligible to win a a drawing for physical fitness de-velopment equipment and oth-er prizes being donated by twin cities merchants.

Youngsters can view some of the prizes to be offered in a window display set up at the

Chapter 18
SEMI-PRO AT ITS BEST

While settling into my new Quaker Oats position I got a call from Sheldon Radom regarding a new semi-pro basketball league based in Michigan, the North American Basketball League (NABL). He was the primary owner of the Twin City Sailors, who were to play in Benton Harbor and St. Joseph, Michigan. I showed interest, so he later visited me at my in-law's house and offered me a contract for $85 per game and a big case of cherries as a signing bonus. I negotiated a per-game salary of $100 and signed right away. I really missed competing in high-level basketball games.

The league consisted of five teams: Twin City, the Grand Rapids Tackers, Pontiac Nationals, Muskegon Panthers and Chicago Bombers. The league's schedule consisted of 16 games, all to be played on Saturday nights to avoid interfering with work schedules.

SAILORS vs MUSKEGON - December 10, 1966

Benton Harbor Sailors,
Semi-Pro League.

I knew many of the players who were going to play in the league. Gary Bradds, Joe Roberts and Mel Nowell had starred at Ohio State. Willie Merriweather, a high school teammate of Oscar Robertson's in Indianapolis, was an All-Big Ten performer at Purdue. Porter Meriwether (Tennessee State), Herschel Turner (Nebraska) and Billy McGill – a former first-team All-America from Utah and the first overall pick in the 1962 NBA draft – were other notable names.

The Twin City team also included former Bradley University standout Al Saunders. My college teammate Jack Egan later signed as well. The league consisted of the best players in the Midwest who were not in the NBA. Keep in mind, with only nine teams in the NBA and very few opportunities to play overseas, some very talented basketball players were available for semi-pro leagues.

I was impressed with the Sailors' talent at our only pre-season practice. The roster also included 6-11 Ernest Jones (a former Globetrotter from Tennessee State), and 6-9 Clarence Ludd, a good street ball player from Gary, Indiana, who played college ball at Prairie View A&M. Larry Comley from Kansas State was a versatile and talented scoring threat and 6-4 guard/forward Bob James from Western Michigan was a crowd-pleasing player.

Our player-coach was Bob Wilkinson, who had been a starting guard on Indiana University's Big Ten championship team as a sophomore in 1958 and gone on to play professionally in the short-lived American Basketball League.

After practice, Wilkinson named the starters. I was truly disappointed that I didn't get the nod but kept it to myself. It was the first time in my life I felt I should have been starting but wasn't.

As a starting guard, Al Saunders got to choose his jersey number. Believe it or not, he picked No. 15, which was my retired number at Loyola. It wasn't even his number at Bradley. I remember asking Saunders if I could wear 15, but before I could explain why, he said "No!"

I don't know how this worked out, but the Sailors had a favorable schedule in the NABL's inaugural season, with 12 of our 16 games at home in Benton Harbor's Colfax Gym. Basketball fans could buy a reserved season ticket for $15 (for 12 games!), while single-game tickets sold for $1 (students), $1.50 (general admission) and $1.75 (reserved). Tickets could be purchased at a number of venues, including the Benton Harbor and St. Joseph chambers of commerce, Radom's Farm Supply and Tacy's Barbershop. It wasn't the NBA, to say the least, but it was good basketball and it paid.

The players arrived early in Benton Harbor before the first game to get better acquainted, and we continued to do so throughout the season. We shot pool and played Ping Pong, cards and other games at Mr. Radom's house. We finished the season with an 11-5 record, good for second place behind Grand Rapids. I was one of the leading scorers on the team and got satisfaction from receiving all-league honorable mention recognition despite coming off the bench. I wasn't pleased, however, to be called "the best sixth man in the league." For me, that was damning with faint praise.

1965-66 CHAMPS

NABL Champs, 1965-66.

We won the NABL championship the second season thanks to the acquisition of my old Loyola teammate, Les Hunter, along with Gary Bradds and Bradley's Mack Herndon. They enabled us to dominate the boards, which combined with our quickness for a lethal combination.

We also had a new coach in Bill Perigo, who did not play. Perigo was another native Hoosier - my Indiana basketball "connections" seemed to be everywhere. He had led Delphi High School to consecutive Indiana state finals appearances in 1928 and '29 and played college ball at Western Michigan University. He later played professionally with the Indianapolis Kautskys and Hammond Ciesars, where one of his teammates was Johnny Wooden. He then went on to coach eight seasons as head coach at the University of Michigan. He was well-known locally, having coached Benton Harbor High School for 13 seasons and winning the 1941 state championship.

I averaged 19.1 points for the championship team. I still didn't start but was always in the game at crucial times.

Although the league was full of talented players, they weren't in great shape. We all had regular jobs, and little time to train. In our case it showed when we played an exhibition game against the Philadelphia 76ers in Benton Harbor prior to our second season. It was "Chet Walker Day." Walker, an

113

All-Star forward for the 76ers, had starred at Benton Harbor High before earning All-American honors at Bradley University.

Chet Walker and his 76ers teammates made up one of the greatest aggregations of talent in NBA history. The Sixers had three Hall of Famers – Walker, Wilt Chamberlain and Hal Greer – in the starting lineup. A fourth Hall of Famer, Billy Cunningham, was the sixth man. The other starters, Lucious Jackson and Wali Jones, were NBA All-Rookie selections. That season (1965-66), the 76ers won the Eastern Division with the NBA's best record before losing to the Celtics in the playoffs. The following season, with essentially the same roster, they captured the NBA title after winning a then-record 68 games during the regular season.

We were competitive for a while, down only six points early in the third period, although in fairness Chamberlain only played half the game. We ran out of gas, though, and Philadelphia pulled away to win, 141-102. Les Hunter, though, never slowed down. He led all scorers with 26 points.

"He was as good as any player on the floor," Perigo told the local newspaper. "I was afraid he would be too good and they would take him with them."

We tied Grand Rapids for the best regular season record (12-4) that season to force a best-of-three playoff. We won the first two games, and neither one was close (140-117 and 131-102). In the clincher, Al Saunders had an off night so I played almost the entire game and finished with 25 points, 11 rebounds and seven assists.

We might have been partially motivated by the all-league selections, announced prior to the playoff series. Grand Rapids placed three players – Nick Mantis, Billy McGill and Willie Jones – on the NABL's All-Star first team. We had one player, Larry Comley, named to the first-team. Al Saunders and Gary Bradds were second-team selections while Bob James made the third team. Once again, I fell into the category of "also receiving votes."

Early the following season, Jack Egan replaced Perigo as the coach. With the team in financial trouble, Perigo resigned rather than take a hefty paycut. I wanted to be a player-coach, but lost interest in that when Egan made me a starter.

Jack Egan named Head Coach
of Benton Harbor Sailors.

The league expanded from five to eight teams and added five games to the schedule in its third season. Egan was a good coach but losing Gary Bradds and Bob James to the NABL's expansion draft was too much to overcome. The Sailors did sign Ron Miller, which meant four of the five starters from Loyola's NCAA championship team – Jack Egan, Les Hunter, Ron Miller and me – were reunited, although Ron only played in a few games before retiring.

We finished with an 11-10 record, tied for fourth in the league. I averaged 21.5 points and was selected to the second All-NABL team. Les Hunter and Larry Comley were on the third team with Freddie Lewis (Battle Creek) and Tom Thacker (Muskegon), both of whom had played for the Cincinnati Royals in the NBA.

The Sailors folded before the next season, but we enjoyed it while it lasted. It was a fun time for Les, Jack, Ron, myself and, sometimes, our wives. We enjoyed quality time before and after games, stopping for meals and reminiscing about our good times together.

One memorable experience occurred when the players and our wives drove home in two cars after a game, but Ronnie got a flat tire. After a long, extended repair, we decided to check into a hotel. I asked the desk clerk, "How much for four rooms?

After he quoted the price, I yelled out, "Wow! Do you have one room for all of us?"

Everybody burst out laughing, and I've never been able to live it down.

I didn't realize it at the time, but those three seasons with the Sailors represented an important transition for me in basketball, even if it was only semi-pro. Had I laid off from competitive basketball for three seasons I might not have been prepared to take the next step in my basketball career.

However, nothing – absolutely nothing – could have prepared me for the most devastating experience of my life.

Chapter 19
SEVERE PAIN

Cynthia Denise was our first born. She was a beautiful angel with a strong grip to go with a heartwarming smile. When she started to make baby sounds, I thought she was saying "da-da." No one would agree with me, but that's how it sounded to her proud father.

Cynthia Denise started to crawl at an early stage in her life and, before we knew it, she was walking. She would fall down but would get right back up and try again. Once she mastered walking, she got into everything. I remember her pouring talcum powder all over herself, playing with the toilet paper, throwing clothes and creating other mischief. When we took her places, she was complimented by everyone for her gorgeous smile, personality and wit.

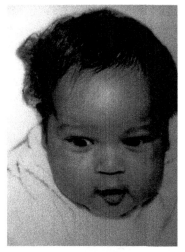

Our first child,
Cynthia Denise Harkness.

When she turned two, however, she started suffering from asthmaticus, a severe case of asthma. Watching this pretty little girl suffer from this was the worst pain I've ever had in my life. I didn't want to see her jump up and down with joy in her crib because I knew most of the time it would trigger an attack. That would devastate me, even though it would subside 10-15 minutes after she took medicine.

In October of 1965, when the wheezing got worse, we rushed her to the hospital. I still have visions of my mother-in-law walking back and forth down the corridor with a rosary in her hand. I can see other family members huddled together with tears in their eyes. I can see others going to the hospital chapel to pray for this sweet, little angel. I see myself looking at her in a large cubical, trying to get her to smile.

The doctors worked and worked on her but to no avail. She died that same day.

I'll never get over that. I think of her all the time.

Cindy playing in her room.

Chapter 20
WITNESSING THE MOVEMENT

The mid-1960s was a time of racial unrest throughout the country, particularly in Chicago. For that reason, Al Raby, a Chicago teacher and civil rights activist, helped entice Dr. Martin Luther King, Jr. and the Southern Christian Leadership Council to come to Chicago. Upon Dr. King's arrival, my then wife, Judy, and her sisters – Kathleen and Loretta – and some of their friends were invited to volunteer in fundraising, recruitment and marching strategies for the SCLC.

Ron Miller's wife at the time, Joanne, also joined the group. She had been arrested some fifteen times for protesting the Vietnam War and Civil Rights issues. Joanne was also one of those who marched across the bridge in Selma, Alabama. I became indirectly involved when Judy hosted a SCLC strategy meeting in our apartment. Jesse Jackson, Al Raby, Minister James Bevel and SCLC executive staffer Jose Williams were among those in the meeting.

I spoke to a couple of them, including Jesse, about my housing discrimination experience on the North Side. Most of the time, however, I stayed in the bedroom, still not really in tune with the movement. I could tell that they were dedicated to the cause, as they strongly voiced their opinions on what different strategies to use. I had no idea they were planning protest marches in all-white neighborhoods such as Cicero, Cage Park and Marquette Park.

The following week Jesse Jackson invited me to a Civil Rights gathering at Liberty Baptist Church, on Chicago's South Side. He told me Dr. King would be the keynote speaker. It was a night I will never forget.

I was so excited that I got there early. I still had a hard time finding a seat, however. After settling in, I made eye contact with Jesse, who was on the podium. Soon after, Jesse got up to the microphone and, to my surprise, introduced me as an All-American and the team captain who led Loyola to the 1963 NCAA championship. He called out my name and asked me to stand up. The next thing I knew, I was receiving a standing ovation that brought tears to my eyes. I had no idea people knew me to that extent. I looked around the church and saw nothing but black people. Those standing close by patted me on my back. I was in awe. I felt as though I was back in Harlem.

A couple of Civil Rights leaders got up and spoke, but my thoughts soon turned to Dr. King. I had only seen him a couple of times on television, on shows such as the one hosted by Irv Kupcinet, a Chicago newspaper columnist who had his own TV talk show. Finally, when Dr. King took the stage, the church rocked! He was mesmerizing. The power of his voice … it was as if he was reciting poetry. I had never heard anything like it before and haven't to this day.

I tried to get Jesse's attention, hoping to meet Dr. King, but they left before the service ended. The impact of his speech never left me, however. There probably were a number of things that led me to change my mind about participating in the Civil Rights Movement, but this experience was the most influential.

Because Ronnie Miller and I were somewhat connected to the Civil Rights Movement through our wives, we were invited to a reception for Dr. King. From the time he entered the room, he seemed to be in control. He complimented the ladies on their charm and told them they looked like beautiful bouquets of flowers preparing to blossom and show off all the colors of the African American rainbow.

He made them feel special, telling them they were the ones in the spotlight at the moment.

He went on to work the room, speaking to people in small groups. He approached Ron and me and said, "Ah, the successful basketball stars." I knew he was somewhat coached by Jesse, who introduced him to us. He congratulated us and, after a little amusing small talk, moved on.

Once again, I was in awe, even though he wasn't as famous then as he would become. I could see greatness in his warm and humble mannerisms. Ron and I will never forget that meeting with Dr. King.

A couple of days later, Dr. King led hundreds of demonstrators to an open house march in Marquette Park. Judy and Joanne marched with them. The demonstrators were bombarded by rocks, bottles, bricks and, as reported by the Chicago Tribune, even a knife. Thirty people were injured, including at least four policemen. Dr. King was among the injured as he was hit in the head by a rock.

Joanne was badly injured by a thrown bottle. Jesse, accompanied by Judy, carried Joanne to a police car that took them away from danger. A paddy wagon finally picked them up and took them up to the hospital. Judy called her mother, Adele Carroll, to retrieve their car, which was still in Marquette Park.

Her mother recruited Jack Todd, a neighbor, to drive over with her. They parked a block away and walked through a crowd of locals, still shouting and throwing objects. Adele and Jack proceeded on, retrieved the car and drove out to pick Judy and Joanne at the hospital. This all happened successfully because my mother-in-law and her neighbor were light-skinned enough to pass for being white. When Judy got home, she told me she had never been so scared for her life because of all the shouting, thrown objects and the hatred she could see in their eyes.

Jesse Jackson, who was named head of the Chicago chapter of SCLC's Operation Bread Basket in 1966, became a good friend of mine. Despite his busy schedule, he played pickup basketball with us at Hales Franciscan High School on Chicago's South Side, where I coached the junior varsity team. He was a good athlete who rejected a minor league baseball contract out of high school to go to the University of Illinois on a football scholarship before transferring to North Carolina A&T. My former Loyola teammates Les Hunter and Jack Egan also came over to scrimmage to stay in shape for the semi-pro league in Michigan. We were all amused while watching Jesse compete with Father Arthur Feldman, a Catholic Priest and the school's athletic director, pushing and shoving for position. Although there were six or eight of us competing in the half court, Jesse's and Father Arthur's determination stood out.

Chapter 21
ABA - NEW PRO BASKETBALL LEAGUE

While reading the newspaper one day in February of 1967, I came across an article about a pro basketball league that was being formed, the American Basketball Association. The new league initially planned to begin with teams in 10 cities within two divisions: New York, Pittsburgh, Indianapolis, Minneapolis and New Orleans in the Eastern Division and Anaheim, Dallas, Houston, Kansas City, and Oakland in the West. A franchise was awarded to Louisville about a month later, and the Kansas City franchise transferred to Denver.

This was a real professional league, with full-time players, that planned to compete against the NBA. I realized then I would always wonder if I could make it at that level. I had not prepared properly to play for the Knicks and was haunted by that failure. I called Les Hunter and told him about the new league, and he was excited as well.

I decided to contact the franchise closest to me, in Indianapolis. I had given a Quaker Oats fitness speech there, so I knew it wasn't too far away, about a 3 ½-hour drive from Chicago. The team didn't yet have front office personnel, of course, so I wrote a letter to the sports editor of The Indianapolis Star, Bob Collins. He later passed it along after the team hired a general manager, Mike Storen, and I was invited to participate in an open tryout in June.

Les and I started working out together, mostly running. When it was nearly time to attend the tryouts, I told my boss at Quaker Oats that I was going to quit to take a chance on this new league. He offered me a small raise, but he knew my mind was made up. Les, meanwhile, contacted the Minnesota franchise.

I was fully aware of the risk I was taking. I could easily fail to make the team and be out of a job. I had a family to take care of and giving up a stable and promising job with Quaker Oats was hardly practical. I just had to try, however.

After I arrived in Indianapolis I met with Storen, who offered me a contract for $16,000 if I made the team. That was $4,000 more than the Knicks had paid me and $8,000 more than the Globetrotters had offered me. The Pacers paid for my room at the Indianapolis Marott Hotel. When I arrived at the tryouts at the Indiana State Fairgrounds Coliseum, 42 guards showed up along with more than 30 forwards and at least 15 centers. And that did not include the other invited players who were staying at the hotel. The big turnout was the result of a well-publicized invitation for anyone interested in trying out for this new professional basketball team. I learned then, there's never a shortage of people wanting to play basketball in Indiana.

I overheard guys saying things like, "Yeah, I tried out for a pro team and got cut in the third round," "I just missed getting to the final cut," or "I was the last one cut." That would be with them for the rest of their lives.

The team was to be called the Pacers, which was announced just before the open tryout. The head coach was Larry Staverman, who had been an assistant at Notre Dame and had played in the NBA and ABL. He was assisted in the camp by Bobby "Slick" Leonard and Clyde Lovellette, former Indiana high school stars who had played for NCAA championship teams and then played in the NBA. They cut over 100 players in two days.

As the number of candidates dwindled, I started thinking about the number of guards who had a no-cut contract. I assumed Roger Brown, who I played against in high school and on the streets of New York, had one. If not, I knew he was a lock to make the team. Freddie Lewis, who I played against in the Michigan semi-pro league, had one and so did Jim Dawson, who had been the Big Ten Conference's leading scorer at Illinois the previous season. Neither of them had to participate in the open tryouts.

That left just two available guard spots. The other candidates included Larry Humes, a former Division II All-American from Evansville College, Hubie Marshall, a standout from LaSalle and two talented local playground legends, Dick Russell and Boo Ellis.

Humes probably was my greatest competition for one of the final spots on the roster. He was from Madison, Indiana and had been the leading scorer on Evansville's back-to-back championship teams. He had been a former high school Mr. Basketball, an award taken very seriously in Indiana at that time.

To say the least, I was worried. I had trouble sleeping in the days leading to the open tryout while going over in my mind how I could make the team.

I also wasn't in the best of shape, something I took pride in. Les and I had worked out but didn't push ourselves the way players do when they're being coached, and the Quaker Oats job and my family obligation prevented me from spending more time on conditioning.

The first practice began with wind sprints. I was happy about that because I had always been one of the fastest guys on my teams. I jumped out to the lead but finished about third. I was in the middle of the pack the second time. After the third run, I became dizzy, walked to the sideline, found a garbage pail and threw up. I couldn't believe my poor conditioning. I didn't play very well in the scrimmages, either. I was a step behind and most of my shots fell short.

At the end of the week the Pacers were going to cut down to the 20 players who would be invited to training camp at St. Joseph's College in Rensselaer, Indiana. From there, the Pacers would make the final cut to 12 players, but I already felt it was over for me.

We were all called into a room, one by one, at the Fair Grounds Coliseum. When my turn came, I walked into a bland room: a desk and two chairs, with no windows. The thought crossed my mind that was to keep you from jumping out after you got the bad news. Coach Staverman told me to have a seat.

"Jerry, I know you're not in the best of shape, but we saw some good things so we're going to invite you to come to Rensselaer."

"I'll do better," I said. "I know my reputation preceded me. Probably, under normal circumstances, I would have been cut."

I was so relieved. I was shaking, with tears in my eyes. Staverman told me I could go out another door if I wished and I took him up on the suggestion so the guys waiting wouldn't see me all teary-eyed.

The guys greeted me warmly at the hotel, thinking I had been cut, but were happy to know I was still alive. It was hard to face the guys who didn't survive. I had gotten close to some of them. All you can say is, "Good luck and let's stay in touch." You really feel bad for them. But you rarely stay in touch.

Getting a second chance was like Loyola all over again, and I took full advantage of it. I worked out in my free time, running three to five miles a day up and down Fall Creek Parkway, near where the Marott was located. Sometimes, I ran to the Senate Avenue YMCA, one of the largest African American YMCAs in the country. I could shoot there and swim a half-mile or mile. At night I did jumping jacks and other aerobic exercises. I rarely went out to parties or enjoyed other entertainment, like the movies or a play. My focus was on preparing to go to Rensselaer.

After the open tryout, the Pacers signed two more former Indiana Mr. Basketballs whom I had played against in college. Jimmy Rayl had set Big Ten scoring records as a guard at Indiana University and had incredible shooting range. He didn't have a guaranteed contract, but certainly had an advantage because of his reputation with the state. Ron Bonham, who could play either guard or forward, also had been a Mr. Basketball. He had been a member of Cincinnati's championship team in 1962 and was the leading scorer on the team Loyola defeated the following year. He went on to win a championship ring with the Celtics but was out of pro ball when the ABA was formed.

The competition for roster spots just kept getting greater.

Finally, training camp arrived in September. On the bus ride up to Rensselaer, the guys talked very little about basketball and much more about music, ladies, cars and clothes. A couple of guys, including Oliver Darden, talked about the stock market and finances.

We started the first practice with wind sprints. The guards and small forwards were in one group and the centers and power forwards in another. I started near the front and stayed close to the leaders until the end, then jumped into the lead. That gave me all the confidence I needed.

During the scrimmage, I pressured the ball from start to finish and never really got tired. The few shots I took were on target and I played really good defense. I even took the ball away from Roger Brown and Freddie Lewis. When I took the ball from Freddie, he looked me in the eyes and said, "Never again." He was right; I never stole it from him again in practice.

On one of the final days of camp, coach Staverman was upset with one of the players who had been pouting. He called me over and told me to defend him all over the court. I said, "Yes, sir!"

I was in his face the entire practice. He hardly got his hands on the ball, much less scored. The player was so frustrated that he left camp, but when management found out they sent someone – Staverman, I believe - after him to talk him into coming back.

After the final scrimmage, Staverman called me in the office and said, "Congratulations, you made the team."

I thanked him, then went to the restroom, locked the door, and cried like a baby. My gamble had paid off, but it had been close. I barely beat out Humes and Marshall for the last guard spot. After gathering my emotions, I called my wife and told her to get ready to come to Indianapolis.

By the way, the pouting player also made the team.

The first Pacer team - 1967-68.

The original Pacers' roster had a definite state and regional flavor. Three players were former stars at Indiana high schools: Ron Bonham (Muncie Central), Jimmy Rayl (Kokomo) and Bobby Joe Edmonds (Indianapolis Crispus Attucks). With the exception of Freddie Lewis, who had played at Arizona State, the rest played college ball at Midwest schools: Bob Netolicky (Drake), George Peeples (Iowa), Oliver Darden (Michigan), Roger Brown (Dayton), Ron Kozlicki (Northwestern), Matt Aitch (Michigan State), Jim Dawson (Illinois) and, of course, me. At age 27, I also had the distinction of being the oldest Pacer, a distinction I never lost. I got my old jersey number back, too – 15.

I was thrilled. I had become a professional basketball player again. I was extremely happy for this opportunity to extend my basketball career, but at the time I had no clue of the impact of my connection to Indianapolis would have on my life.

Now that I had made the team and been joined by my family in Indianapolis, it was time to find an apartment.

I looked through the newspapers for some leads. Those that looked like a good match, I called to set up appointments to see in person. When I arrived at the first one, the person showing the apartment was cold and uncooperative.

When I called some others, I was asked bluntly if I was "colored." When I said yes, they said no units were available.

Oh no, not again, I thought.

Frustrated, I called the Pacers to vent my problem. I was put in contact with Bill McGowan, a real estate representative, who showed me a place close to downtown on Pennsylvania. It was nice and it was available, but it was not what we were looking for. We tried the new Meadows Apartments near 38th Street and Meadows Drive on the city's northeast side, close to the Coliseum where the games would be played. The folks there were upset because a lady had been approved for an apartment. She signed the contract, made the down payment and took the keys. Then the Meadows' officials found out that, although she was white, her husband – my Pacer teammate Matthew Aitch - was black. As far as they were concerned, they had met their quota. I was turned down although they had several openings.

The same area is predominantly black now.

There was another opening in the vicinity further north, but I was turned down again because Oliver Darden and his wife, Rose, already had been accepted. Another quota had been reached. I didn't know it at the time, but Oliver and Rose got the apartment only after Oliver threatened to file a lawsuit.

Finally, I heard back from McGowan. His friend, Robert V. Welch, an influential business and civic leader, directed him to a diverse townhouse community on 38th and Post Road. We went to look at them and liked them a lot. When I looked at the name of the apartments, I felt secure. It was a R.V. Welch development.

It also helped that my in-laws in Chicago, the Carroll family, knew Father Mike Mooney, a Chicago Catholic priest born in Indianapolis. Father Mike's brother was Bill Mooney, president of Mooney-Mueller-Ward, wholesale pharmaceutical firm. When we got to Indianapolis we had great support and friendship from the Bill Mooney family which – like Bill McGowan and Bob Welch – helped us settle in Indianapolis during some trying times.

Chapter 22
MAKING MY MARK

I played well as a reserve early in the Pacers' first season and I was confident and determined to help the team. I showed that desire as we warmed up before a road game early in the 1967-68 season. One of my teammates wasn't throwing the ball back to me to take my warmup shots. When I brought it to his attention, he said, "You're not starting."

I said, "So what? I want to be ready when I get to play!"

The next game was on Monday, November 13, against the Dallas Chaparrals in Dallas. I played sparingly in the first half. Late in the fourth quarter, Freddie Lewis – who had scored a team-high 26 points – twisted his ankle and had to come out of the game. Our coach, Larry Staverman, put me into the game but right away one of the Dallas guards drove around me and scored an uncontested layup.

"Come on, Jerry, let's go!" Staverman shouted.

I thought to myself, *Okay, I just got in here.*

Bob Netolicky scored on a swooping, across-the-middle hook shot to tie the score. Roger Brown hit an 18-footer to put us up two points with 1:45 left in the game. The Chaparrals player-coach, Cliff Hagan, scored on a one-hander to tie the score with 1:10 left to play. I brought the red, white and blue basketball down the court and passed it to Oliver Darden, who bounce-passed the ball into Neto. Bob tried to get to the basket but was stopped by John Beasley. Neto passed the ball out to Jimmy Rayl, who passed over to Roger for a medium-range jump shot. Roger's shot glanced off the rim and Dallas rebounded with 32 seconds to go.

The Chaparrals took their time down the court. The sparse crowd – only about a thousand fans showed up that night – started yelling, "Go Chaparrals, go! Go Chaparrals, go!" Dallas passed the ball around. Finally, with six seconds to go John Beasley took a jumper from the corner. Neto said later he

I played well as a reserve.

nicked the ball, but it still dropped through the basket. With just two seconds remaining, Dallas had a 118-116 lead.

I had no idea the remaining seconds would become a defining moment in my professional basketball career. In my life, in fact.

Oliver Darden took the ball out of bounds and flipped it to me, just couple of steps inbounds. I took a short step and sailed the ball over my shoulder toward the basket. The ball was still in the air when the buzzer went off, and the fans were still cheering Beasley's basket, thinking they had won the game. Their radio announcer, Terry Stembridge, was screaming, "Dallas wins!"

I watched the ball start to descend about mid-court, and then saw the net move. It had hit the backboard and gone through! The arena, full of cheering a fraction of a second earlier, fell stone-cold silent. The fans stood with their mouths wide open, stunned by what they saw. I was equally stunned. My teammates ran toward me yelling, screaming and hugging me. I looked at referee Joe Belmont, who was running toward the scorer's table.

It has to be good, I thought. *We're in overtime.*

Belmont signaled that the basket counted. And then, to my surprise, he began to run off the court. The game was over. Even the players were startled at first. None of us – especially me – remembered that it was a three-point shot. Final score: Pacers 119, Chaparrals 118.

The three-point shot had been an innovation of the American Basketball League in the early Sixties, and the ABA had revived it. But most three-pointers were planned, normal basketball shots from just behind the three-point stripe on the court – not a desperation, court-length bomb. But didn't matter if the shot was a half-inch behind the line or at the other end of the court, it counted three points.

Staverman later told Stembridge he walked off the floor twice that night, first as a loser and then as a winner. Stembridge recalled that his declaration, "Dallas wins!" turned out to be the most premature journalistic announcement since that famous 1948 headline in the *Chicago Daily Tribune*: "DEWEY DEFEATS TRUMAN."

People sometimes ask me how many times I've viewed the replay of that shot. I can answer in all honesty, none. Absolutely none. Pro basketball had not yet caught on in Dallas, and there were no newspaper photographers or television cameras around at the end of the game to record the moment. There are no pictures, film or anything else, just the memories of the people who were there.

The Pacers got a call from a representative for Joe Garagiola's television show the next morning asking me to fly to New York to appear on the show, but that was soon canceled. I couldn't get from Dallas to New York in time, as we had a game back in Indianapolis two nights later, and the lack of visual evidence caused the show's producer to lose interest.

I couldn't sleep in my hotel room that night. Darden and I stayed up all night talking about it. Ollie said, "Jerry, do you realize you hit the longest shot in basketball history and you won the game with it? It had to be at least 90 feet. I could not believe it when it went in. Do I get an assist for that?"

We laughed. Ollie dozed off but couldn't stay asleep. He was as excited as I was.

Later he said, "Jerry, did you forget for the moment that it was a three-point shot? Did you see Cliff Hagan telling his players they should have been playing better defense?"

We laughed some more, and I said:

"Ollie, I hope Freddie (Lewis) is all right, but I'm kinda glad he sprained his ankle."

We couldn't stop talking about it, couldn't stop laughing about it.

"Jerry, did you hear Staverman say he has never seen anything like it?"

"Ollie, you know sometimes I think I'm blessed. But let me get some sleep, we got an early plane to catch. And, yes, if I were the scorekeeper, I would give you an assist. Now, get some sleep!"

The shot was originally reported as a 92-footer. However, later measurements confirmed it was "only" 88 feet. A baseline-to-baseline measurement of a basketball court is 94 feet, but basket-to-basket is 90 feet. I took a short step and dribble before I let it go. Although record-keeping on shot lengths is a bit shaky, it was believed to be – and was reported to be – the longest shot during a regulation basketball game.

When the team arrived in Indianapolis, Dick Denny of *The Indianapolis News* met us at the airport and interviewed me, and a photographer took pictures of me posed with Lewis, Darden, Ron Kozlicki, Bob Netolicky and Bobby Joe Edmonds.

Teammates help me celebrate what was, at that time, the longest shot in history.

At the next game at the Coliseum, General Manager Mike Storen brought in a member of the United States Marine Corps color guard, Sergeant First Class Jerry Schuler, to pin a sharp-shooter medal on me prior to the opening tip-off. The fans gave me a wonderful ovation. I went back to the bench, this time really feeling good about myself, feeling needed and wanted. When I went into the game, whenever I got the inbound pass to take the ball down the court, people started yelling, "Shoot, shoot it from there."

My shot was later recognized in a Ripley's Believe it or Not cartoon, and the ball was sent to the Naismith Hall of Fame for display.

The Pacer fans had taken to us early. At most home games, if we won, a group of us would meet with fans in a small restaurant in the Coliseum to have a snack and discuss the game. We

I was pinned with a Sharp Shooter medal.

had an unusually close relationship with them, and I always enjoyed our conversations. That night, they went on and on about my shot.

Over the years, many Pacers fans have told me they were there the night I hit the 88-footer – in the Coliseum in Indianapolis. After a while, I stopped telling them it happened in Dallas. Let them have their memories, however skewed.

It's always been said records are made to be broken. And on February 17, 2001 – some 34 years after my shot – Baron Davis of the Charlotte Hornets buried an 89-footer at the end of the third period of a playoff game against the Milwaukee Bucks. The shot still stands as the longest shot in professional basketball history. I joked with Baron at a conference for former ABA and NBA players about his shot.

"It was luck, but what can I say? Records are made to be broken," he said.

I reminded him that, while Charlotte won the game, my shot was the game-winner.

Posing some 35 years later when Byron Davis broke my record.

Although the history of "longest shots" can be a bit dicey, the sport has done a better job of documentation in recent years. But there is proof of some long bombs before recent times.

Before Davis's shot, the Chicago Bulls' Norm Van Lier had the longest-recorded NBA shot of 84 feet against San Antonio in 1977. LeBron James hit an 83-footer in the second half of a game against the Boston Celtics in 2007.

I was at the game in Indianapolis when Pacer Herb Williams hit an 81-footer on January 8, 1986. I'll never forget because some fans turned to me and yelled that Herb got my record. I was relieved later when the final measurement was announced. After the game I asked Herb if he was going for my record. He smiled.

In 1963, Boston Celtics' legend Bob Cousy was credited with a 79-footer against the Syracuse Nats. In 2007, I saw Detroit's Rasheed Wallace bank in a 62-footer to tie the game in regulation play. The Pistons went on to win in overtime, 113-109.

Although not the longest, one of the more memorable bombs was Jerry West's last-second 55-footer in the 1970 NBA Finals between the Lakers and Knicks. Under today's rules, West's shot would have given the Lakers the win. West tied the game but New York went on to win in overtime, 111-108.

The longest shot on record in college or pro basketball is 89 feet, three inches, tossed in by Les Henson of Virginia Tech against Florida State in 1980. The shot gave Virginia Tech the victory, 79-77. Prior to that you have to go back to 1955 when University of Alabama forward George Linn hit one from 84 feet, 11 inches against North Carolina.

For high schools, it will be hard to beat the effort of Chris Eddy from Fairview High School in Pennsylvania. On Feb 25, 1989, with his team trailing Iroquois 50-49 in Erie, Eddy hit a desperation shot at the buzzer to give Fairview the win. The heave was measured 90 feet, two inches.

The longest shot made by a female at any level is believed to be the 80-foot buzzer-beater by Nikki Fierstos in 1993. Fierstos, a 5-4 junior from Manchester (Indiana) High School, nailed her guided missile in the consolation game of a tournament at Huntington North School. But, Lake Central still won the game, 80-61. Neither the Indiana High School Athletic Association nor the National Federation of State High School Associations keeps track of long shots, so the "record" appears to be hers.... until someone can prove otherwise. Like myself, Nikki Fierstos has been recognized by the Guinness Book of World Records.

By the beginning of the new year in 1968, the ABA was gaining traction and the Pacers were one of its premier teams. We led the new league in home attendance and maintained that pace throughout the season.

A few days before the start of the regular season, the league announced Indianapolis would be home to the first ABA All-Star game at Butler University. For me, the highlight of the game was that my old Loyola teammate Les Hunter, now nicknamed "Big Game," made the first of his two All-Star teams. I got to spend some time with Les, including a nice dinner. I don't remember the details of our conversations, only that it was wonderful to reminisce. I do remember Les telling me about all the "goodies" the All-Star players received: shaving kits, gym bag, clothes, caps, sneakers, coupons for gasoline, cologne, food baskets and color television sets.

The All-Star game only added to my positive feelings about the ABA and its chances of survival. The Pacers had opened the season back in October with a 117-95 victory over the Kentucky Colonels, a game for which more than 2,000 fans were turned away. My old New York rival Roger Brown scored 24 points to lead the scoring.

I only scored five points off the bench, but I was ecstatic afterward. For the first time, I felt like a professional basketball player. I hadn't lasted long enough with the Knicks to have that feeling.

We got off to a great start because of our organized training camp and pre-season. We were 11-2 in November and 18-7 early in December. The bottom soon fell out, however, as the other league teams caught up with us. A seven-game losing streak dropped our record to 18-14, and we split the next two games.

Given our struggles, Pacers fans probably weren't giving us much of a chance when it was announced Freddie Lewis was out with the flu for our game with the New Jersey Americans on Dec. 26. I got my first start in a major league professional game that night and responded with 21 points and eight assists in a 117-107 victory.

That personal highlight didn't give us a spark, unfortunately. We continued to struggle, and as the 78-game regular season wore on my body began to rebel. I had never played that many games in one season, not even close. The ABA's curious scheduling didn't help. It wasn't unusual to play games on three consecutive nights in three different cities.

As the season progressed I lost some of my speed and jumping ability. My knees began to hurt, and then my back became sore as I tried to baby my knees. I didn't have a guaranteed contract, so I didn't complain; I just tried to hide it. To make matters worse, I came down with the mumps and missed two weeks in mid-February.

I returned for the stretch run and we made the playoffs despite a losing record (38-40). We got swept, 3-0, in the first round of the playoffs by the Pittsburgh Pipers, led by Connie Hawkins, the league's regular season MVP. The Pipers went on to win the first ABA championship, beating the New Orleans Buccaneers in the finals.

Despite the disappointing finish to the season, I had a lot of reasons to be happy. The Pacers had led the ABA in attendance and had a solid fan base. I felt as if I had a secure place on the team and was settling into the community. I got an off-season job with the YMCA Fun Mobile, which provided recreational activities in various parts of the Indianapolis inner city and enabled me to engage in one of my favorite activities: working with young people.

I was really optimistic at the start of my second season with the Pacers.

I received a $1,000 raise, but more importantly we traded for All-Star center Mel Daniels from the Minnesota Muskies. Mel had been the league's leading rebounder, the Rookie of the Year and the runner-up to Hawkins in the MVP voting. The Muskies were having major financial problems and needed cash immediately to finance their move to Miami, so they reluctantly agreed to trade Daniels to the Pacers, who scrambled to raise the $100,000 necessary to complete the deal. Mel was a great talent, but also a fierce competitor who came to play every time he took the floor.

The players voted Mel and me co-captains before the season began, which pleased me a great deal. But although we were regarded as a championship contender, we just didn't jell at the beginning of the season. We lost seven of our first eight games, and coach Staverman was replaced by Bobby "Slick" Leonard, who had helped with the open tryouts before the first season. A native of Terre Haute, Indiana, Slick had starred on Indiana University's 1953 NCAA championship team and played seven seasons in the NBA. He also had coached the Chicago Zephyrs and the Baltimore Bullets in the NBA. Although his NBA coaching record was far from impressive (44-78), he had worked with young players who lacked experience.

I scored two as Reggie Harding looks on.

While Staverman had been a quiet coach, Leonard was far more flamboyant and boisterous. He took over the reins at a tough time. Staverman had won his last game, in Los Angeles, to improve our record to 2-7, and we were in the midst of a 10-game road trip that was broken up into segments of three and seven games, with a break between. After a few eye-opening practices,

I started in Slick's first game as head coach in Minnesota against the Pipers. Minnesota Pipers? Typical of early ABA franchise shuffling, the Pipers had moved from Pittsburgh despite winning the first league title to replace the Muskies, who moved to Miami.

The knee and back problems from the previous season were beginning to return, but I kept them to myself because I was playing well. Over a six-game span from October 31 to November 7, I averaged 12.6 points per game, with games of 17 and 16 points. I had scored 11 points by the third quarter in Slick's first game at Minnesota when I tried a shake-and-bake move on Chico Vaughn and felt my back go out. The pain was incredible, as if someone had stabbed me. I didn't return to the game and was sent home for treatment while the team continued the road trip.

I rejoined the team for practice before its first home game in 23 days, against Dallas. Slick put all the guards on the line to run a "suicide." That consists of running from the end line to the foul line and back, then half court and back, then the far foul line and back, and finally the other end line and back. I believed I could beat all the guards but I also thought, *let's take it easy.* I didn't want my back to go out, so I finished dead last in the drill.

I didn't get into the game against Dallas until about a minute remained. I knew that wasn't a good sign. When Slick finally called for me to report, for the first time in my life I didn't want to play. It wasn't that I was embarrassed, it was that I knew I was about to get cut and I wanted to protect my scoring average. I had averaged 10.2 points over my nine games and I knew playing in this game would drop my scoring average below double figures. But, you do what the coach says. I scored right away but didn't get another attempt before the end of the game. My average dropped to 9.2.

I didn't play in the next game two nights later, a victory over Los Angeles. By then my fate was obvious. Mike Storen called me in to his office the next day to give me the bad news - the Pacers wanted to put me on waivers. I told Mike I didn't want to play for any other team and might as well retire. I thought it was unfair to let me go while I was recovering from an injury, but I couldn't do anything about it. Pro basketball is a business and I was a replaceable part.

My ABA career was over after playing in 81 games - just 10 in the second season, which had started with so much promise.

Mike Storen was good to me, though. He gave me some college scouting opportunities and paid me much more than what scouts were getting at the time. I also was able to work on some of the television broadcasts as an analyst, which was a good experience for me.

The Pacers have continued to treat me well over the years, especially my old New York playground rival, Donnie Walsh, who became their general manager in 1986. I played with so many talented young men, including two – Roger Brown and Mel Daniels - who went on to be elected to the Naismith Hall of Fame, and made lasting friendships. My ABA career was short, but it fulfilled a dream and created many connections that are with me still today.

To play and become friends with some of the best on and off the court is something special.

Chapter 23
AFTER BASKETBALL

It wasn't long before the Greater Indianapolis United Fund (later renamed the United Way of Central Indiana) called and offered me a job.

Once again, I would be breaking new ground as its first African American fundraiser. One time in 1971, Dick Fague, the top executive who hired me, called officials in Carmel, an almost entirely white community north of Indianapolis, to see if it would be all right to have an African American work there. They said yes, so my territory was expanded to include Carmel and Noblesville, another predominantly white suburb. After a year or two, I was promoted again to a new position, the director of minority affairs.

Ltd United Way program.

I staffed an excellent minority committee made up of community leaders, and we came up with the following programs:

- Leadership Training and Development (LTD): preparing minorities to serve on boards of directors.

- Minority Vendor Fair: minority vendors showcasing their product to United Way Agencies.

- Minority Key Club: consisting of minorities who gave from $1,000 to $25,000 to United Way.

- Volunteer Breakfast: collaborating with Indiana Black Expo to recognize outstanding minority volunteers from not-for-profit agencies.

Also, a paid position was created for a minority intern each summer.

I stayed with the United Way more than 25 years and really enjoyed speaking and promoting community agencies. Many of those agencies helped me when I was growing up in Harlem.

In 2018, the United Way of Central Indiana celebrated its 100th Anniversary. To my surprise and great honor, I was asked to be the Grand Marshall of the Future United event at the Indianapolis Motor Speedway.

Summer intern selection.

Minority Recognition Breakfast.
Speaker Danny Glover with
Mary Hardin.

Breakfast Chair Helen Clay with Comedian Sinbad.

I was Grand Marshall for United Way in 2018.

Chapter 24
A CALL FROM CHANNEL 13

While at United Way, a local television station called to offer me a sportscasting position. At the time, its call letters were WLWI and it served as the ABC affiliate for the Indianapolis market. About midway through my tenure there, the station changed its call letters to WTHR and, a few years later, switched its network affiliation to NBC. To avoid confusion, I'll refer to the station as Channel 13 or TV-13

Although I had no experience, I agreed to give it a try. Television stations in the city were under pressure to hire minorities at the time and I would be the first black to be hired at TV-13 – and one of the first black sportscasters in Indiana.

I began by working as a reporter on the urban beat and then moved to the sports department. Before long, I was the weekend sports anchor. I was awful at first, and I knew it. I stayed up late at night, even though I still had my full-time job with United Way, to practice. I'd look in the mirror and read

One of my first assignments

Associated Press and United Press International copy aloud. I began to improve, but I was never fully satisfied with myself.

One of my weekend co-workers was a weatherman by the name of David Letterman. Yes, that David Letterman. Sometimes after the early evening newscast we would go out to eat together. Then we would pitch pennies (closest to the wall wins the pennies) before the later newscast. After that we occasionally would go to the Broad Ripple area of Indianapolis – where David grew up – and enjoy a soda or two.

Letterman had the same sense of humor that later would make him famous. At that time weathermen had magnetized numbers to place on maps to show various temperatures. One time all of the numbers began falling off the board, prompting Letterman to say, "Oh-oh, ladies and gentleman, we are under attack, temperatures are falling all over the state of Indiana at a fast pace." We all laughed out loud on the set.

A good friend from the TV13 Days - David Letterman.

He really was a nice guy and continued to be after gaining national fame. Whenever I was going to be in New York, he would leave tickets for my wife, Sarah, my Aunt Clara and I to attend the taping of his show. The last time we went I was taken into the "Blue Room" to sit with all the VIP guests.

For a short time in 1973, I was part of a history-making group at Channel 13, when African Americans filled every weekend anchor position. Renee Ferguson was the news anchor and Capt. Joel Wilkerson from nearby Fort Harrison did the weather while I anchored the sports. It probably was the first time that had happened in the country. Although it was never talked about, I was truly proud of that.

After eleven years on the job. I began to receive criticism from the TV-13 sports director, who was not happy with my on-air performance. I felt pressure from that, and it had a negative effect on my work. I always had a problem dealing with criticism. I tried to make up for the criticism the only way I knew – by hustling harder. I began covering two, and if possible, three high school basketball games on weekend evenings while other stations would at best cover one game.

I also did Loyola Basketball along with anchoring weekend sports on TV13.

Throughout my tenure there, I was able to break news because of my connections. For example, in 1971 Roger Brown called and told me George McGinnis – a sophomore at Indiana University at the time - was going to sign with the Pacers. I called the sports director and he broke the story.

I also covered the historic NCAA championship game between Indiana State and Michigan State in Salt Lake City in 1979. Larry Bird wasn't talking to the media at the time, but after his team lost the final game I asked my former Pacers teammate, Mel Daniels, who was an ISU assistant coach, if he could get Larry for me. Mel asked, but Larry refused at first. He remembered me sticking a microphone in his face to ask about his thumb injury before his trip to the Final Four. Mel kept asking, and Larry finally agreed. When he walked over, I apologized for the earlier incident. He nodded slightly and conducted the interview. We had no satellite trucks then, so we had to send the tape of the exclusive interview via overnight mail back to Indianapolis.

Larry never used it as an excuse, but I don't think he was fully recovered from his hand injury when he played against Magic Johnson and the Spartans in the championship game.

I also had a degree of exclusivity with Indiana coach Bob Knight. He had gotten into an argument with Channel 13's sports director and banned him from covering IU's team. I was called on to fill in. Knight was very cordial in our first meeting. We talked off-air about the Loyola-Ohio State game in which we played against one another in Columbus early in my junior season, in December of 1961. The Buckeyes were the nation's top-ranked team and we were undefeated (5-0) to start the new season.

"I recall how overly aggressive you played in that game," I told him, smiling.

"Ah, we did win, didn't we?" he said.

They did, 92-72. Looking back at old news clippings, I noticed Knight was scoreless in that game and I led Loyola with 20 points. I probably wouldn't have mentioned that had I known at the time, though. It's always interesting how paths cross in basketball.

Afterward, Knight said I was welcome to come down anytime for an interview. I told him I appreciated that, and he patted me on my back before leaving.

Another incident that stands out with Knight occurred in 1979, one of the more infamous episodes of Knight's colorful career. He coached the USA Pan American Games team to a gold medal in San Juan, Puerto Rico. During his time there, he was accused of assaulting a Puerto Rican policeman and was roundly criticized for his lack of sportsmanship during the final game. The next day, a Saturday, I went to Bloomington to get his side of the story. I was the only sports reporter there. We talked for a good ten minutes. I led the newscast with the exclusive story and left additional clips for the sports director.

During my television career I was surprised how many people knew me from my time in basketball. Tennis star Jimmy Connors, for example, agreed to an interview with me after a match in Indianapolis. He waited patiently for about seven minutes before we could get a feed from the station. He had grown up in Illinois and was aware of Loyola's NCAA championship, so we had a nice conversation about that.

Another athlete had to wait nearly ten minutes to record an interview with me. We had crossed paths a couple of times when I was a young teenager and saw him with his father. He lived about ten blocks from me in Harlem. I later saw him again at his high school, where Loyola practiced for the NIT. And we had spoken at Chicago Stadium during one of those college double- or triple-headers. I thanked him for waiting after we finished the interview and he said, "No problem. We're both from Harlem."

His name: Kareem Abdul-Jabbar.

Another time I was among five reporters waiting to speak to another New Yorker. He saw me with my microphone and said, "Jerry?" When I confirmed, he pulled me from the crowd and took me and the cameraman into a room where he gave me an exclusive interview.

His name was Lou Carnesecca, the longtime coach at St. John's University and, for three seasons, head coach of the ABA's New York Nets. It was heartwarming for "Looie" to do that, especially since one of my television competitors in Indianapolis, Channel 8's Chet Coppock, was also there. I chuckled about it, but I liked Coppock a lot.

I also covered the Indianapolis 500. It's rare to see African Americans at the Speedway, and especially so in those days, but the drivers treated me well, especially Johnny Rutherford, Mario Andretti, Art Pollard and brothers Al and Bobby Unser.

One time I took a helicopter to Bloomington for a game between Indiana and Army. Coach Knight had a press conference after the game, but I wanted to talk with him one-on-one.

When I approached him, he said, "Not now. I have a friend from Army waiting."

I responded that it would be short.

"Did you hear me?" he said.

"But Coach, we got the helicopter running because of the weather. We're afraid it won't start up again if we shut it down."

"Well, that's your problem, I got people waiting for me."

I had no choice but to wait. Finally, he came over for the interview and again bawled me out. But we did it and the cameraman and I raced off for the helicopter. While in the air, we radioed Channel 13. There was no way we could get back in time to put the interview on the air, so we decided to transmit it without the game highlights. That was, in a way, my fault. I should have covered the press conference, knowing how Coach Knight could be. I thought our relationship was good enough that I could get a one-on-one interview, especially after he told me I could get him at any time. He probably meant any time he was free.

Purdue's All-America center, Joe Barry Carroll, was strongly protected by his coach, Lee Rose. Carroll and Rose always allowed me to interview him, though, although rarely with other media members present. I often wondered why. I do know Joe Barry always felt relaxed with me. That came in handy when Joe Barry led the Boilermakers to the 1980 NCAA Final Four at Market Square Arena in Indianapolis.

I felt obligated to cover stories of interest to members of the black community but didn't want to overdo it. For example, I covered the Dust Bowl basketball tournament, an inner-city playground event, sometimes referred to as Indy's version of New York's Rucker Park tournament. The tournament got its name from the courts where future stars such as Oscar Robertson honed their skills before the courts were paved.

I also covered Golden Gloves boxing and legendary boxing coach, Thomas "Sarge" Johnson and events such as the Naptown Muscle Contest, a weightlifting and body-building competition at the Wheeler Boys Club.

I covered Crispus Attucks High School's football team when it had not won a game. I had some of the players in tears talking about their season, but they were full of determination. I was there when they won their first game. I loved track and field, so I covered Indianapolis Public School students in that sport, for both Channel 13 and WTLC radio.

I used "Sweet Georgia Brown," the Harlem Globetrotters theme song as background music while giving sports scores on television and sometimes had former Globetrotter Hallie Bryant (a Crispus Attucks alum) live on Channel 13 to perform tricks with the basketball.

I also frequently covered Kevin Merriweather's girls' AAU basketball teams when girls' sports were fighting for recognition.

During my time on the urban beat, I covered Civil Right issues with authority and confidence. In 1970, I covered a sit-in by students at Marian College (now Marian University), a small Catholic school in Indianapolis. The students, mostly African Americans and members of the school's Union for Black Identity (UBI), were protesting policies and procedures they believed to be inadequate and, in some cases, racist. Joe Smith, a Marian student and founder of UBI, later became a prominent Civil Rights leader in Indianapolis.

On another occasion I virtually took over a news conference featuring the wives of local and national Civil Rights leaders. Mrs. Ralph Abernathy, Rosie Brown of the Indianapolis Urban League and several others complimented me on how I helped run the news conference.

I also had my share of on-air bloopers. The worst of all was when I was describing an injury to Pacers guard Warren Jabali. I reported he had a slipped disc in his back, but pronounced "disc" without the "s."

People later told me they couldn't believe what they heard, saying, "Surely, he didn't say that!"

But I did. Oh boy, did I ever.

It's easy to smile about it now, but it took me a while to live down that one. Most broadcasters will tell you that they can report or anchor flawlessly and never hear a word from the public. However, make one mistake and you won't hear the end of it.

When the sports director was on vacation I often filled in on weekdays. That required me to rush from my full-time job with United Way over to Channel 13. Mark Harmon, who eventually took my place on weekends at 13, would write some of my script and I would finish the rest when I arrived at the station. On one occasion I wasn't able to get to Channel 13 until 15 minutes before the newscast began at 6 p.m. I sat on the set for the opening shot, then rushed downstairs to the sports department to finish typing the script and then rushed over to a technician to pick out and time highlight videos.

I was in a bind and I knew it. When I gave the director a copy of my script and went to the set, I knew I did not have it together. Early in my segment, I froze. Just froze. I didn't say anything for what seemed like several minutes. It was actually only about five seconds but that's a virtual eternity of "dead air" in the broadcasting business. It seemed as if everybody on the news set also froze, looking at me, wondering if I'd ever start talking again. I finally composed myself and finished the sports segment.

I ran to the director during his break and said, "I hope it didn't look as bad as I felt."

He said something like, "I've seen worse."

I was providing the color commentary on Channel 13 for the championship game between the Pacers and Los Angeles Stars in 1970, in Los Angeles. After the Pacers clinched the series in Game 6, I was told to rush into the locker room without a headphone to interview the champs. I couldn't hear a producer, so I talked with Roger Brown, Freddie Lewis and team president Mike Storen. I never got a wrap-up or stop cue, so I just kept going. I must have talked to the entire team before somebody finally came in and stopped me.

I interviewed Bill Cosby at halftime of that same game. Fans began to converge on us as we talked until we were crammed together. "Can't you see we're trying to do an interview?" Cosby said.

All he could talk about was Brown, who capped off a great series with 45 points in the final game. "Did you see that move that almost left the defender on the ground?" he said. "He can pass, too!"

I then asked Cosby when he would be coming back to Indianapolis. "I don't know, the last time I was there I was stopped by the police in my rental car and I was treated badly," he said.

I quickly went to another question before turning it back over to the anchors. Everybody said I handled that delicate situation well.

I was happy to be a black pioneer in the sportscasting industry, especially in Indianapolis. I would be remiss if I didn't include Chuck Workman in that category. In 1974, Chuck was named sports director at WTTV, the first African American in the state to hold that position. Chuck, who passed away in 2012, was a fine sportscaster but I think most people in Indianapolis remember him as an announcer and promoter of jazz music. Chuck is in the Indiana Pioneer Broadcasters Hall of Fame and the Indiana Jazz Hall of Fame.

As I look at my career, I realize that I interviewed former Pacers Lenny Elmore, Clark Kellogg and George McGinnis, as well as former Indiana University star Quinn Buckner. They all became standout black broadcasters in later years.

I was released from Channel 13 after 12 years but still maintained a strong presence on the broadcasting scene in Indianapolis.

Late in my TV-13 tenure I attended a major African American function. I don't recall which one, specifically, but out of nowhere the late Al "The Bishop" Hobbs, a local gospel radio personality, told the audience WTLC-FM (107.5) was going to ask Jerry Harkness to do a morning sports show. Everybody applauded. I was tickled to death the black community responded that way.

WTLC was founded in the late 1960s when a group purchased radio station WAIV, changed its call letters to WTLC, and switched its music format from classical to jazz and rhythm and blues. Throughout its history, WTLC has provided an important voice for blacks in central Indiana. I truly enjoyed my stay there, working with people such as "Super Jay" Johnson, Tony Lamont, Gene Slaymaker, Roger Holloway, Tim Johnson, Kevin Bradley, "Sparkle Socks" Griffin and Ricky Clark.

It was much easier for me there than at Channel 13. Everybody was so positive and warm. I was part of an award-winning morning news team. I started a high school athlete-of -the-month award, which went to one who excelled in sports, academics and community service. The award was called the "Bob Jewell Award," named after a former Crispus Attucks High School basketball player who won the 1951 Arthur L. Trester Award for mental attitude in the state tournament.

Jewell, who worked at Eli Lilly when I was at WTLC, offered commentary in monthly interviews about character, academics and effort. I also interviewed and awarded a plaque to the monthly winner.

I talked with Dr. Frank Lloyd Sr. about the Bob Jewell Award at a meeting of the 100 Black Men of Indianapolis. He very much liked the award and what it stood for but wondered why the award went only to African American students.

My answer: "Yes, we need to emphasize blacks in academics, especially to our predominantly black audience."

Kevin Bradley, colleague at WTLC Radio.

He understood but thought opening it up to the entire community would give more prestige to the award.

Dr. Lloyd was one of the most influential black leaders in Indianapolis history. A physician, he retired as president and chief executive officer of Methodist Hospital. He was a member of numerous civic organizations, including the White River Park Commission, the United Way and the Greater Indianapolis Progress Committee. He was one of the founders of the Midwest State Bank, the 100 Black Men of Indianapolis and, oh yes, WTLC-FM. Suffice to say, when Dr. Lloyd spoke, I listened. During my stay at WTLC, we gave out about 20 awards, four of which went to white athletes.

I also began a "Prediction of the Week," in which I forecast the winning high school team of a big Friday basketball game. I developed audio sound effects as if I was floating out into outer space to get my answers, and it was very popular.

I also remember recording interviews with prominent sports personalities, such as Julius Erving. I joked around with "Dr J" and asked him what he'd do in a basketball match-up against one of the WTLC disc jockeys, let's say Tony Lamont. He responded with something like, "Tony, I will mop you up," or "I'll dunk on you." Some famous athletes were creative in joking about what they would do to Tony. The audience loved it.

Chapter 25
INDIANA BLACK EXPO

Dr. Martin Luther King Jr. and the local president of the Southern Christian Leadership Conference, Reverend Andrew J. Brown, were good friends back in the 1950's. Dr. King would preach at St. John's Baptist Church and after the service the two men would spend time together developing strategy for a civil rights movement.

Dr. King introduced Operation Breadbasket to Reverend Brown. It was developed to include a civil rights movement and economic arm of the SCLC in Atlanta in the late 60's. Operation Breadbasket fought poverty and employment discrimination. This led to the possibility of having a Black Expo. Rev. Brown sent four ladies to Chicago to explore the Black Expo there. They were Phylis Carr, Mary Logan, Barbara Wilson and Helen Perkins. They reported that Chicago Expo was more of a business expo than anything, and suggested we take a family approach. Reverend Brown's next step was to put together a board with James Cummings as President, Holton Hayes as Vice President, Emma Johnson as Secretary and W.B. Ransom treasurer. The staff through SCLC consisted of Bill Crawford, Glen Howard and George Vansickle.

Among the various committees organized was a professional basketball game committee. I wound up co-chairing the first Black Expo Southern Christian Leadership Conference NBA-ABA basketball game along with Hoyt Diamond at the Fairgrounds Coliseum in 1971. Roger Brown, Mel Daniels and Darnell Hillman participated, representing the Indiana Pacers. Others included Connie Hawkins, who received the MVP award, John Brisker, Rick Barry, Tiny Archibald, Charlie Scott, Julius Erving, and Warren Jabali. NBA veteran and Pacers guard John Barnhill was one of the coaches. Oliver Darden selected the game's Most Valuable Player. We were able to get regional television coverage, with Bill Russell providing commentary.

Despite the fact we were novices, the event went over very well. We had more than 3,000 fans in attendance and it was the first time NBA and ABA

Volunteers from first Black Expo. I'm in the top row, 2nd from right.

players competed together in a game on television. The network affiliates offered us $8,000. We negotiated for more but to no avail. I had them send the check directly to the SCLC in Atlanta. We also sent about $9,000 from proceeds from program advertisements and gate receipts.

Jesse Jackson gave encouraging remarks at the first Indiana Black Expo luncheon. The keynote speaker was John Mackey of the Baltimore Colts. The beauty pageant, art gallery and concerts led by Donny Hathaway, the Dells, and Honeycombs all were excellent and the booth spaces were nearly full.

We conservatively estimated the attendance at 50,000 spectators. The volunteers at the wrap-up meeting a week or so later were overjoyed when we learned how successful Expo had been; some were in tears. It was a joy for me to see the black Indianapolis community come together to make this huge project a success. Democrats, Republicans, Urban League, NAACP, Black Panthers, Black Radical Action Project, WTLC, the *Indianapolis Recorder* newspaper, local fraternities and sororities, Urban Union, and churches all collaborated.

For the second Expo, I researched the history of African American music in Indiana. I really enjoyed meeting people who took part as entertainers and remembered those who had passed but had contributed so much before them. I had pictures taken with the Hubbard Family; Wes Montgomery; one of the original Ink Spots; Noble Sissle, one of the writers of the Butler University fight song; Larry Ridley; and the Hampton Family.

I had more than 100 pictures put on display and gave all of them to Black Expo before I left.

The second NBA-ABA basketball game was played at Nicoson Hall at Indiana Central, which is now called the University of Indianapolis. We did not get a TV contract, but we sent SCLC a donation of about $10,000 from our gate receipts. A suggestion was made that we were pocketing some of the proceeds, but we were not. I greatly resented that and decided I was finished with the game. I would never take money, period. Along with Hoyt Diamond, Gerry Williams and other volunteers, I had worked hard on the game.

Later in life, I thought it was perhaps selfish of me to quit the committee because I had gotten angry. I'm not proud of that, but that's the way I was. Black Expo successfully put on another game before ending the series in 1972.

Indiana Black Expo continued to grow with the addition of the Circle City Classic football game and the black circus, among other events, and became a nationally recognized event. I was proud to have had a small part in it.

The start of the first Indiana Black Expo at the State Fair Grounds.

Chapter 26
COACHING

I coached my son, Jerald, in YMCA basketball and then Catholic Youth Organization (CYO) basketball at St. Luke Catholic School, where we won a number of championships. I also coached my daughter Julie's team to a basketball championship. Julie did not lose a game in her final middle school year, going undefeated in basketball, kickball and volleyball.

Judy, my ex-wife, also coached Julie and stayed on top of our children's academics and extra-curricular activities. She was always at the school, checking with the teachers. As a result, they both did extremely well. My parents never saw me run track or play basketball, so I made sure I attended as many of Jerald's and Julie's games as possible.

One of my close friends, Hoyt Diamond, and I joined up to coach some high school teams in Amateur Athletic Union (AAU) basketball. We traveled to Florida, won a single-elimination tournament, and advanced far in an AAU tournament. We also won a local Dust Bowl tournament in Indianapolis. Once again, talent was key to our success, but Hoyt's coaching skills also came into play. We had a diverse group of young men. It's always exciting when I run into some of the players I coached. Now, they introduce me to their wives and their children and I can tell they are doing well.

Both Julie and Jerald attended Cathedral High School, where Jerald played freshman basketball before quitting to focus on his studies. As a senior at Cathedral he was named one of the presidents of his class. Julie made the varsity volleyball team as a freshman and the basketball coaches could not wait to get her as a sophomore. Both were in honors classes.

St Luke's City Champs Team.

Coaching talented AAU team.

Chapter 27
THE DANCER AND FILMMAKER

One day, Julie came to me and said she didn't want to participate in sports anymore. I was shocked. I had looked forward to her receiving a scholarship for basketball and watching her play. I knew she would be good enough.

"Then, what do you want to do?" I asked.

"Dad, I think I want to dance."

Here she was, 14 years old. I always thought dancers usually started at six or seven years old. Hurting inside, I asked, "Are you sure?"

She assured me she was. I suppose like most "jocks" I didn't believe anyone trained harder or more seriously than a person involved in competitive sports. I soon learned how naive I had been.

Julie began training at the Jordan dance studio on the Butler University campus. Whenever I attended her practice I saw a few dancers her age, but most of them were younger. I could tell, though, that she loved it.

She was so determined that she trained in our basement after coming home from practice. I would hear her singing and dancing so I'd run downstairs to catch her in the act, but she would stop before I got to the bottom steps and smiled. We played that game for the longest time. I heard tunes from "My Fair Lady," "The Sound of Music," "Hello Dolly," and "West Side Story," but I could never catch her in the act.

After her junior year she tried out for Walt Disney Productions in Florida. It was her first tryout for an event outside of Indianapolis. Competing against hundreds of people from around the country, she made it! We went to Florida to watch her perform and my father, who joined us, got teary-eyed. She was outstanding.

Julie attended Point Park College in Pittsburgh for dance and graduated magna cum laude. She performed in several plays and dance shows there and

Walt Disney Productions.

then went to New York for another major audition. Once again, she made it: to my amazement she was now a Radio City Rockette, only the third African American member of that legendary dance line at Radio City Music Hall. During her ten-year career there she also became a Rockette spokesperson.

When Julie was trying to make the dance squad for her tenth year, the competition was becoming increasingly younger and more talented. She trained so hard she lost a lot of weight, much more than necessary. I was a little worried that she wasn't eating right. She grew dizzy during this ordeal, maybe even passed out. I always thought she got that drive and determination from her mother and my mother.

"Babes in Toyland" performance with the Radio City Rockettes.

Finally, the day came and, once again, she made the team. The instructor's first advice to her was to go out and get a big steak and some wine.

Since her Rockettes career ended, Julie has enjoyed an active and varied career as an entertainer. She was a dancer/singer with Jimmy Buffet's traveling show. She performed in plays, including Broadway productions of "The Will Rogers Follies" and "Hello Dolly." She has also appeared in films, including Tom Hanks' directorial debut, "That Thing You Do!" as a member of The Chantrellines.

She even wrote a monthly article for *"Dance Spirit,"* a national dance magazine. You just never know. Teamwork, practice, competitive spirit and endurance ... what's good for basketball also applies to other disciplines such as dance. Incidentally, while performing with the Will Rogers Follies, she met President Bill Clinton, Hillary and Chelsea, so I wasn't the first one in the family to meet a President.

Julie lives in Los Angeles, where she is an entertainment reporter for "Made in Hollywood." She interviews actors, actresses, directors and other filmmakers about upcoming movies. She also provides a weekly movie review on L.A. television.

She and her husband, David Arnold, an excellent comedian, have two daughters, Anna Grace and Ashlyn.

Julie meets President Clinton, his wife Hillary, and daughter Chelsey.

Sarah and I visited my daughter and family in California. Front row: left, Anna Grace, and right, Ashlyn. In the back row are David and Julie.

While at Indiana University, my son Jerald directed and produced a documentary on college fraternities and sororities called "Steppin" – the title coming from "step shows," an African American art form with cultural roots in African dancing. He introduced "Steppin" at the Walker Theater in Indianapolis and it brought the house down. It was excellent, and that wasn't just Dad's opinion.

Gerald's Documentary "Steppin" received high praise.

After graduation, Jerald produced an episode for the ESPN Sports Century series on Al Unser Sr. of the auto-racing world and a documentary on Hoosier basketball standout Damon Bailey. He also produced a special on Queen Latifah, a documentary called "Facing the Façade" about African American students at Indiana University, a documentary on the Indianapolis Recorder, (Indianapolis' African American newspaper) and an episodic bio on the Bee Gees, just to name a few.

He also directed and wrote a documentary that gave new life to our 1963 Loyola team and, in particular, our landmark game against Mississippi State. The film is entitled "The Game of Change," which, thanks to Jerald, is how the game itself is now often referred: The Game of Change.

Jerald and his wife, Barbara, also have two daughters, Kara and Kiley.

As other parents know, it's difficult to express your pride in your children's accomplishments.

Jerald Harkness in his studio.

Jerald and his famiily - wife, Barbara, and daughters Kara and Kiley.

Chapter 28
100 BLACK MEN OF INDIANAPOLIS

The founding members of the 100 Black Men of Indianapolis were some of the city's most prominent citizens. Listed below are most of the founding members in 1984 who received a charter from 100 Black Men of America. The goal of the 100 is mentoring based on the slogan "What They See is What They'll Be."

100 Black Men of Indianpolis.

- Dr. John Joyner
- Moses Gray
- Reggie Bishop
- Dr. Frank Lloyd, Sr.
- Sam Jones
- Dr. Lehman Adam
- Rev.Landrum Shields
- Dr. George Rawls
- Dr. Freeman Martin

Also, in 1984, yours truly, Moses Gray, and Charles Williams, our first Executive Director, started developing or supporting the following programs.

- IPS Mentoring Program
- Summer Academy
- Douglas Little League Baseball

Soon after, the 100 Black Men Organization added the following:

- Beautillion Militaire (Co-sponsor: Jack N Jill of America Indianapolis Chapter)
- Black History Challenge
- Scholastic Basketball
- 100 Black Men Medical Program
- Jerry Harkness Award
- Wellness Program
- 100 Track and Field

Dr. O.T. Gordon, Murv Enders, Clarence Crain, Glen Holbrook, Acey Byrd, Ontay Johnson, and James Duke's leadership continued to make our chapter one of the best in the country as programs for Financial Literacy, Collegiate 100, and Robotics were added.

Beautillion Militaire.

Chapter 29
BLESSING IN DISGUISE

There was this high school student growing up in Arkansas in the early 1960s.

One day he was watching a college championship basketball game. The game was close and exciting. Late in the second half, one of the teams battled back from 15 points down to tie the game and go into overtime. Then, on a last second shot, that team won the game. At that time there were not many African Americans portrayed in a positive light on television and here were four starting players of color on the team – Loyola – winning a national championship.

That youngster was the second-leading scorer on his high school team but watching that championship game motivated him to want to do more than just go to college. He wanted to help his people. After receiving his college degree, he went on to medical school and became a doctor. He later landed at Methodist Hospital in Indianapolis, specializing in gastroenterology, the branch of medicine that focuses on the stomach and digestive system.

Dr. O.T. Gordon, Jr.

I found out all of this because Dr. O. T. Gordon, Jr. became *my* doctor. But that's not the end of the story.

During one of my routine check-ups, he found cancer in my colon. He immediately directed me to Dr. Frank Lloyd Jr. who performed a six-hour surgery to remove a portion of my colon and correct a hernia problem. I was cancer-free.

Dr. Gordon and I became good friends, especially while volunteering in the Indianapolis chapter of the 100 Black Men of America. He later became the President of the 100 Black Men of Indianapolis while I was the Executive Director. During our time of service, we were selected as the best chapter in the nation in our category. After speaking to representatives in the national office in Atlanta, I was told we were the best overall in all categories.

Dr. Gordon and I also went into a successful athletic shoe business. After about seven years, Dr. Gordon took his share of the profits and moved back to Arkansas with his family, while I stayed in the business for a total of 15 years.

Just think, he was influenced to go to medical school by a basketball game in which I played and end up finding cancer in my body and saving my life. It turned out to be one of my greatest connections.

Chapter 30
THE RAJAH

My boyhood rival and Pacers teammate Roger Brown was deep into his own bout with cancer in 1997. This once-great athlete, a future Hall of Famer, had become frail and you could see the illness in his eyes. Roger, though, had charisma, that certain laugh and smile. He didn't lose that even when he was in serious pain.

Once during his final days, he called me and said, "Guess who called me?"

"Who?"

"Bill Cosby."

"What did he want?"

He laughed and said, "He was checking to see how I was doing and he wanted to tell me how much he liked my game. He went on describing some of the moves I made. We had some small talk and then he said, "If you need anything, call me."

That's how popular Roger Brown was.

Roger was a difficult person for people to get to know, but once he trusted you he was a great friend. That was evident one time when we brought some former Pacers together to sign red, white and blue ABA basketballs outside my Athlete's Foot store downtown. Roger, Mel Daniels, Freddie Lewis, Tom Thacker and Bob Netolicky all attended. The customers bought the basketballs from me and then got in a long line for signatures. As the guys took a little break and stood up to stretch, I could see Roger was in a lot of pain.

Rajah

I said, "Roger, you didn't have to do this."

"What are friends for?" he said.

I'll never forget that moment.

After we finished signing basketballs and autographing other memorabilia, we all went to Ruth's Chris for dinner. When Roger was spotted among us, we were told everything was on the house. Roger, with that small laugh and grin, really liked that. "Everybody has been so nice," he said.

A week later, I went to the home of his ex-wife, Jeannie, where he was confined to bed in his dying days. He was so weak that Mel Daniels had to carry him around. I sat by his bed and prayed. He passed away a few days later, only 54 years old. His funeral service was at Market Square Arena, the Pacers' home arena. Former Pacers and local dignitaries visited his casket at midcourt. Jeannie asked me to give the prayer as part of the ceremony.

The first high school game of my life was played against Wingate and Roger Brown. We became teammates as professionals and lived in the same city after retiring. I was thrilled that he ultimately got what he deserved by being inducted into the Naismith Basketball Hall of Fame in 2013.

A few years after winning the 1963 NCAA Championship, Les Hunter, Jack Egan and I thought we had the ingredients to make a movie based on our experiences. A television producer who met with Les really liked the idea but could not sell it to her boss. Years later, Jack and I met with ESPN representatives in Chicago but did not hear back from them.

MOVIE

In January 2006, the movie "Glory Road," opened in U.S. theaters and topped the box office the first weekend of its release. The film was based on the true story of the Texas Western University team that won the 1966 NCAA basketball title with an all-black starting lineup, defeating an all-white team from Kentucky. I thought it was a good story, especially for the black community.

Texas Western Basketball Team 1965-66 NCAA Champs. *Courtesy of Texas Western University Athletic Department.*

167

Everywhere I went, African Americans were talking about the movie. I probably got an extra dose, living in Indianapolis. As home to the quarters of the NCAA, there were several special events associated with the release of the film.

I enjoyed the film but thought a story about an integrated team such as ours would be better, especially one that helped bring about racial harmony and justice in our landmark game in the tournament against Mississippi State. I don't know if it would have sold as many tickets as "Glory Road," but it would show what can be accomplished when we work together.

Texas Western's NCAA championship did destroy one school of thought, the idea that a basketball team needed at least one white guy to keep the black players in line. Jack Egan told me some white people told him during our championship season, "You guys are doing really well, Jack. But without your leadership, they would be so disorganized, faltering all over the place, running wild."

Jack said, "All the plays and leadership come from the center position. Les Hunter makes all the half-court decisions on what plays we should run. We are confident, so confident in Les's play-calling skills."

Egan always said it with a straight face and then watched as the white guys walked away, scratching their heads. We still believe a movie about Loyola will come about.

Jerry Harkness and Harry Flournoy, who was on the Texas Western
Championship. Flournoy told me there would be no
Glory Road without the Game of Change.
Courtesy of Photographer Carl Black.

Chapter 31
DAD

I found out later in life that my dad had a special bond with his brother and sisters. They had pledged to help each other financially and emotionally during difficult times. My dad basically decided to help them instead of us. He didn't have the means to support both and he saw my mom had acquired a boyfriend after they split up, so he chose them.

My dad did help me while I was in college by sending me $15 every month. We got to know each other a little better whenever I visited New York and I really enjoyed our time together. He later met and loved my second wife, Sarah. He always wanted to talk about my basketball career and very little about our past.

I wish I had spent more time with my father and mother. When my sister, who did a yeoman's job taking care of my dad in his later years, called to tell me we were losing him, Sarah and I immediately caught a flight and rushed to his hospital bedside in New York. As he lay there with his eyes closed, I spoke to him periodically. He would look at me occasionally, but he could not respond. I believe he was able to recognize me.

I felt good when the nurses told me how proudly he talked about me. I spoke at his funeral, and I knew in my heart I had forgiven him. I just wish I had known him better.

Chapter 32
GAME OF CHANGE REVISITED

During March Madness, I often get phone calls from reporters looking for a different angle on the tournament.

One year the former Mississippi State captain, Joe Dan Gold, and I were interviewed via a three-way call by a reporter about the Mississippi State/ Loyola-Chicago game. After the interview ended, Joe Dan and I stayed on the line to bring each other up-to-date on our lives since the game. We discovered we had a lot in common. We both loved working with children. He was a school administrator and I was a mentor, and we both were connected to the Big C (cancer). I had been operated on for cancer twice (thyroid and colon) and he was being treated for colon cancer. We both liked the idea of going out on a speaker's tour about the history surrounding the game.

We spoke on the phone a couple of times after that to get better acquainted. He told me about his former teammates, Red Stroud and Leland Mitchell. Stroud was very sick and Mitchell was paralyzed from the neck down. The Loyola team by that time had lost Vic Rouse and Jim Reardon. We considered all of them to be good people.

I told Joe Dan that my son, Jerald, was working on a documentary about the Loyola-Mississippi State game and would be getting in touch with him. Joe Dan said he looked forward to it.

Jerald was really excited about the project. His first interview was in Red Stroud's home and he was treated like royalty, sharing a wonderful meal with them. The interview went well, but Red clearly was ill. A short time later, Red passed. The first thing that came to my mind was how well the Stroud family had treated Jerald. I wished Stroud and I had spent a little time together during our college basketball all-star games.

Jerald wanted to have Joe Dan and me meet at my house in Indianapolis and be interviewed together and individually. We agreed to it, so after some

40 years we met again. We reminisced and laughed for hours. It was really a nice get-together. We talked again about going on a speaking tour, especially now that a documentary was in development. After that meeting we spoke on the phone, but I didn't see Joe Dan again until the debut of my son's documentary, "Game of Change," during the 2009 NCAA Final Four in Detroit.

I know I mentioned this in a previous section but I'm sure you'll forgive a proud father for redundancy. The title of Jerald's documentary – "The Game of Change"– has become synonymous with the game itself. It truly was a game that brought about change.

Joe Dan and Jerry Harkness, 2009.

Team members and dignitaries from both schools were present for the documentary's 2009 premier. I was particularly happy to meet Martha Colvard, the widow of former Mississippi State President Dr. Dean Colvard, who pushed hard to get approval for the team to go to the 1963 NCAA tournament. It was a pleasure to see the Mississippi State players again, too. All of them were warm and cordial, and it made me wonder how they could be that way after growing up in a racist environment that stereotyped blacks.

One of their players told me his father had been a Ku Klux Klan sympathizer, but later helped care for an elderly black couple. I always wanted to discuss the issues between the two races in greater detail, but there were always more positive things to talk about.

Mississippi State team.

The Mississippi State players from that team were a unique group. They all achieved their college degrees, and none of them had been divorced. Many were strong followers of the Lord, especially center Bobby Shows, who founded a ministry called "Sports Crusaders" that works with young people.

Shows' wife, Jane, and my wife, Sarah, became acquainted on the bus ride back to our hotel. Upon arriving there, Jane told Sarah she had something for her and to come by their room when she got a chance. Jane later gave her a "365 Daily Devotional Book" entitled "Jesus Calling." Sarah was very appreciative and could not wait to get back to our room to tell me how

nice and thoughtful that was. I found out later that Bobby had received national recognition for his spiritual and youth basketball work.

One day I realized I had not spoken with Joe Dan Gold in a while, so I called his home and found out from his wife Rosemarie that he was at a conference. She gave me his phone number and told me, "Give him a call. I know he'll be glad to hear from you."

Joe Dan

I contacted him right away and we both talked about how fortunate we were to have such wonderful life experiences. We both agreed on how blessed we were, especially with our wives. I did not have any idea that it would be our last conversation. A few months later, in April 2011, I received a telephone call from a reporter, telling me Joe Dan had passed.

I was shocked. I had known about Joe Dan's battle with cancer but thought it was under control. He was always jovial, warm and upbeat and never let on how serious his condition might have been. We had discussed our cancers on several occasions but always slid over it to talk about our experiences with youngsters, family, and the possibility of getting together to tell our shared story.

Two services were to be conducted for Joe Dan, one in West Liberty, Kentucky, where he spent his later years, and the other near his hometown of Benton in western Kentucky. As I wondered if I should attend and who I could go with, I received a call from author Mike Lenehan, who was writing a book on the 1963 Loyola team. We had spoken before, but he wanted to talk to me again about the Loyola experience. I agreed if he would drive me to Kentucky for Joe Dan's funeral service, and we made the trip together.

Along the way I began to realize how much I was going to miss Joe Dan. We had become good friends, with so much in common despite the difference in our backgrounds. Both of us had been team captains, which helped us throughout our lives. We had children and cared about other peoples' children, too. He expressed that interest as the superintendent of a school district.

His teammates agreed he had been a consistent player and superb team captain who complemented coach Babe McCarthy. In fact, when McCarthy left Mississippi State in 1965, he recommended his assistant coach, Joe Dan, as his replacement. Joe Dan took over as the Bulldogs' head basketball coach at age 23 and coached them for five seasons.

He had a great sense of humor, too. He said, for example, the Loyola players had intentionally broken his hand so he could not play against Bowling Green in the NCAA regional consolation game.

When Mike Lenehan and I arrived at the church, I immediately went to a room to change into a suit and tie. As I walked into the sanctuary, I looked around and saw the church was full ... with white folks. I was the only African

American in attendance. I looked up front and saw Joe Dan's wife, Rosemarie. As I walked toward her she mouthed the words, "Thank you. Thank you for coming." As I got closer I said, "I know Joe Dan would have come to mine."

She introduced me to Joe Dan's son, John Douglas, and other family members. Hugs were exchanged and our eyes filled with tears. I told Rosemarie I had no idea he was so sick. "I know," she said. "He kept it a secret. That's the way he was."

I then noticed a photograph of Joe Dan and me shaking hands before the "Game of Change" was sitting just to the left of the casket. Looking at Joe Dan's face in the casket, tears began to flow. Shifting my gaze between the picture and his body in repose was just too much for me. I looked away and saw all his college teammates and Mississippi State officials in the front row.

"Game of Change" hand shake.

One of them was Hall of Famer Bailey Howell, who had been a first team All-America for Mississippi State in the late 1950s and gone on to a stellar NBA career as a six-time All-Star and two-time champion with Boston. Howell's experience illustrated how white players also were victims of segregation. He had led Mississippi State to a 24-1 record and the SEC championship in 1959. That team could have won a national championship, but the university declined an invitation to the NCAA tournament to avoid playing against black players.

Bailey walked over and shook my hand. Then someone touched me on the shoulder and asked me to follow him outside the sanctuary. There, he asked me if I would be an honorary pallbearer. I said, "Yes, it would be an honor." He then pinned my lapel with a red carnation. When I got back into the sanctuary, the Gold family waved me over. They wanted to take a picture of me with the family. I hesitated because I wasn't sure how that would look to others in the church, but it went well. I then sat down in an empty seat in the row behind his teammates.

The music was different than what I was accustomed to hearing in my church, Eastern Star Baptist Church in Indianapolis. It had a country flavor, and I truly liked it. Bailey Howell spoke eloquently during the service, and then Joe Dan's pallbearers and teammates gathered. All of us were wearing dark suits and a red carnation.

I felt like a member of the Bulldogs team at that moment, helping lead Joe Dan to his resting place, and it was a great feeling. Back on the road toward home, I thought how ironic it was that God had reunited me with Joe Dan Gold – this time in an environment where nobody thought of race or color.

Me with the family of Joe Dan Gold at his funeral.

Chapter 33
COLLEGE HALL OF FAME

Everybody in the Loyola of Chicago basketball world was overjoyed when, in the spring of 2013, it was announced the 1963 team would be inducted into the National Collegiate Basketball Hall of Fame.

The honor was all the more special because we would be the first team inducted. It was appropriate, because we had played so well together. I was the leading scorer, but on any given night any one of us could have played a starring role. In my three years on the varsity, we never had controversy because someone was being selfish. I used to hate it when the opponent played a zone defense because I was not that great an outside shooter, but I was able to get the ball to Miller, Egan or Rouse to break the zone. When we played in a team member's hometown, such as East St. Louis for Rouse, we tried to set him up more so he could stand out for his family and friends.

Shortly after the Hall of Fame announcement I received a call from an executive with the Hall of Fame, asking me to come to Kansas City to represent the Loyola team during the induction ceremonies in November. "You mean, none of the other players would be there?" I asked.

He told me Les Hunter, who lived in Kansas City, was the only other player being invited.

"Look, we're all in our Seventies," I said. "It was a team effort and we would like to enjoy this major award together."

He said travel expenses were the major issue. I told him I just couldn't do it, because everything we accomplished had been as a team.

"Well, you were the captain and you represent the team," he said.

I told him that while I appreciated the honor, I simply couldn't do it. After I hung up, I called Les Hunter. We were on the same page. He also had refused the offer.

A couple of days later I received a call from someone at Loyola telling me the university had worked out an arrangement with the Hall of Fame. All the team members and some university staff members could attend the induction ceremonies. Knowing the character of my teammates, they would have taken the same stance as Les and I did.

With all the publicity we received in 2013, Herm Hagan – a teammate in my early years at Loyola – read an article about the Game of Change in his hometown Las Vegas newspaper. Learning I was living in Indianapolis, he somehow reached my ex-wife, who

Basketball Teammate Herm Hagen and wife Judy.

gave him my phone number. I was so happy to hear from him, and suggested we get together.

My wife and I flew to Las Vegas two weeks later, and Herm met us at the airport. After introducing him to Sarah, he made all kinds of gestures indicating how fine he thought she was while she looked away. We always had done that when we were dating girls in college, but this time he went overboard.

We went to dinner that night with him and his wife, Judith. Afterward, Herm and I went outside by his pool, listening to oldies-but-goodies songs and bringing each other up to date. It turned out he had traveled all over the world while in the service, playing basketball and enjoying the ladies in every port. He had become a successful businessman, and recently had retired from corporate management to spend more time with his wife.

Near the end of our long conversation, I told him the Loyola team was going to be inducted into the National Collegiate Basketball Hall of Fame in Kansas City and that he should join us. After some hesitation, he agreed.

I contacted Loyola officials handling tickets for the events, who said he would have to pay for his own expenses, but he could be with us. When I called Herm with the information he said he would call to make a reservation, but then told me he had severe heart problems and was taking ten pills a day. I told him I was doing the same.

"Yeah, Jerry, but I only have ten percent of my heart working," he said. "I cannot sleep in a bed. I have to sleep upright in a chair."

"Oh, you look good to me," I said. "Just call the lady tomorrow. Everybody would love to see you, okay?"

The next afternoon, I called the Hall of Fame officials to see if Hern had called. He had not. "Darn him", I thought. "Let me give him a call."

I called and his wife, Judith answered. I asked if Herm was in. She said, "Herm died in his sleep last night." I could not believe it! She calmly said, "He had a heart attack. You know, he only had ten percent use of his heart".

Still shocked, I said, "Yeah I know".

They flew him back to Chicago and I spoke at his funeral. "It was nice how God got us together one more time to bring us up-to-date with each other," I said.

The Loyola team joined a distinguished group of individuals at the induction ceremony. players Xavier Daniel (Wichita State), Marques Johnson (UCLA), Tom McMillen (Maryland), Bob Hopkins (Grambling State), and coaches Gene Keady (Purdue) and Rollie Massimino (Villanova). George E. Killian and George Raveling were inducted for special contributions to basketball. Houston's Elvin Hayes, a previous inductee, also participated in the ceremony.

College Hall of Famers.

While in Kansas City, a few of us got a chance to visit the Negro Leagues Baseball Museum. The history there was eye-opening. I also was happy my daughter, Julie, and her husband, David, were able to join us.

During the 50th anniversary activities surrounding the Game of Change, the 100 Black Men's office in Indianapolis received a call from a man wanting to speak with me. I didn't recognize the name, so I assumed it was another person passing on congratulations. The office manager, Vernice Williams, told me she thought he was a doctor.

"You don't know a Doctor Jeremy Lazarus?" she asked.

I didn't recognize the name but decided to call him back. The conversation went like this:

"Hello, yes, may I speak to a Dr. Lazarus?"

"Yes, speaking."

"Dr. Lazarus, this is Jerry Harkness returning your call.

"Oh, Jerry, congratulations. I have been hearing and seeing all of your accomplishments on television and in the papers. That's how I tracked you down."

"Oh, thanks."

"You don't remember me, but I'm the person who accepted you and your family into an apartment on Winona Avenue in Chicago. Then, when you came to get possession of the apartment, I told you that it had already been rented out.

"Oh yeah, that's when your father had rented it out."

"That's what I'm calling about. I want to sincerely apologize for that entire situation. My father was not quite ready to do the right thing. I am so sorry for what I did. It had not been rented out."

Nearly 50 years had passed since I tried to rent that apartment after moving to Chicago to work for Quaker Oats. He seemed sincere, so I accepted his apologies. He then invited my wife and me to his inauguration as the president of the American Medical Society. We accepted, and after the festivities were able to talk with him briefly. He told me he had just met President Obama about health insurance and had a lot of other items on his agenda. I wanted to tell him we were going to meet the President, too, but changed my mind.

Talking with friends later, some of them said I shouldn't have accepted Dr. Lazarus' apology. Perhaps he only had done so because he was going into a prestigious position and didn't want any negative publicity to come back on him.

My life experiences told me otherwise. Consider the 1963 Mississippi State players. They wanted to play against African Americans in the NCAA tournament but the politicians in their state and others didn't want that to happen. I felt Jeremy Lazarus wanted change but his father, who had to deal more directly with the outside world, wasn't ready to face the consequences.

Think about it. The guilt had weighed on Jeremy's mind for a long time, and now he was apologizing for his father, for the community, for how everything was at the time. Now he was a doctor, ready to lead all the physicians in America. I had no doubt he would do a good job.

Among the landslide of reunions in recent years was one for the Real Harlem Basketball Players in 2015.

There, I talked with fellow Patterson Projects resident Tiny Archibald. I hadn't spoken with him since the 1972 Indiana Black Expo all-star game in Indianapolis, when Tiny was at the peak of his Hall of Fame career. He and Julius Erving won the awards for that game as the game's outstanding player and the most valuable player, respectively.

Tiny told me and my childhood buddies, Elbert Shamsid-Deen and Wally Hassan, that he watched us play on numerous occasions in the park and at P.S. 18 John Peter Zenger, both of which were located in the projects. Tiny said he picked up a lot of pointers from our play.

Archibald and me

The three of us were in awe. Really? Tiny Archibald picked up pointers from us?

"Yeah," he said, "I pulled away a number of how-to from you guys."

I said, "Man, I don't know if you're pulling our legs, but we got our chests sticking way out."

He laughed.

There's another connection. We lived in the Patterson Projects in the Bronx, went to Dewitt Clinton, we are left handed and had similar basketball skills. We thrived in up-tempo games, shooting from 10 to 15 feet or driving to the basket. We differ in that Nate could also shoot the long ball and give it up with split second accuracy.

He truly was one of the greats of the game, a six-time All-Star who started for Boston's championship team in 1981. He's perhaps best known for being the only player in NBA history to win the scoring title (34.0) and assist title (11.4) in the same season, in 1972-73.

I tried to figure out if he was telling the truth by comparing our ages. Tiny is eight years younger, so he would have been about ten years old when he saw me play in the projects. Perhaps it was true.

When Tiny received his award for outstanding community service for mentoring and other contributions, I felt another connection. God has made it possible for me to win many awards, but there's something about winning an award where you grew up. You're able to share it with guys from 60 years earlier who helped you become the ballplayer you turned out to be. I also was happy to see members on my father's side of the family from Pennsylvania in attendance.

I received a plaque at the event, but didn't read the inscription until later:

"Real Harlem Basketball Players Award presented to Jerry Harkness. Harlem Born, Harlem Legend, Ground Breaker, NCAA Division I Basketball Champion, College All-Star, Basketball MVP, Role Model and Mentor."

That pretty much sums up the parts of my life of which I'm proudest. Then somebody whispered in my ear that I was the first team captain from Harlem to win an NCAA title.

I started thinking about my mom, who was there through all my difficulties. She was there when I was turned down by all those colleges, she was there when we lost our first-born, she was there when I was cut by the Knicks and couldn't find a job. She was always there to inspire me to stay out of trouble and to display perseverance. I now realize whatever determination and inner strength I have, I got from Mom. That night in Harlem ... I knew she was there, too.

In 1992, Milton Harrison, the longtime President and CEO of the Newark YMWCA, founded the Sports Legends program, which brought together former professional athletes to motivate and inspire youngsters in the Newark area.

Joking with former Baseball standout Tony Oliva and former great Jim Marshall in Milton Harrison Legends Program.

Milton Harrison and me.

Over the next 13 years I attended several of the annual events, which included visits to local schools and a dinner to raise funds for scholarships. I was able to mingle with some of the greats from a variety of sports, but I made a special connection with John Carlos. He won the bronze medal in the 200-meter dash at the 1968 Olympics in Mexico City, but is most famous for his demonstration on the medal stand when he and teammate Tommie Smith, who had won the gold medal, wore no shoes and black socks and bowed their heads while raising a black-gloved fist during the playing of the Star-Spangled Banner. It was their way of protesting the unequal treatment of blacks in American society.

I have always respected the bravery of Carlos and Smith and the sacrifices they made to promote justice and equality. That moment in Mexico City is still discussed and debated, and likely will be for years to come.

But there was another reason I made the connection with Carlos. He, too, is from Harlem. It was easy to converse with him about our common upbringing. We talked about going to the Apollo Theater and the incredible performers who appeared. We talked about the Colonial Pool, where we both swam at least three times a week in the summer. Like Carlos, I lived about a block or two away from the public pool, we both got to be a pretty good swimmer. When I swam against the guys at YMCA and the Harlem Boys Club, I won almost all of the time.

Tommy Smith, Jerry Harkness and John Carlos.

Naturally, the conversation turned to track. We talked about running at Randalls Island in Public Schools Athletic League (PSAL) meets. And, when he talked about stealing food from the train tracks at the 155th Street bridge to give to the poor, I knew exactly where he was talking about ... not too far from Yankee Stadium.

Legends myself, Connie Hawkins and John Carlos.

Other topics of our conversation included The Palladium, where we showed our stuff in dances like the mambo, cha-cha, and pachanga; the Audubon Ballroom; Sweet Daddy Grace; the Abyssinian Baptist Church; the Harlem Y and the Calypso Ballroom on 110th Street. It's funny, but I bet as kids John and I were in the same place on numerous occasions. We both went to Frederick Douglas Junior High, although he's five years younger.

It was wonderful to relive those memories together, memories of people, places and events which were still so vivid after 50-plus years, especially with a legendary athlete such as John, who took a stand for what he believed in.

As I was sitting in my living room trying to put this book together, I got a call from Doug Elgin, the commissioner of the Missouri Valley Conference (MVC). He congratulated me because I had been selected to be inducted into the 2016 MVC Hall of Fame as an "Institutional Great." I thought, "Are you kidding me? That's awesome." But I was even more impressed that the commissioner called to break the good news. When I got off the phone, I told Sarah and she was more excited than I was. Then I thought, "Here I am, 75 years old, and still being recognized. That is pretty neat."

It was also a bit ironic because Loyola didn't join the MVC until 2013. Loyola was an independent school (no conference affiliation) when I played. Adding to the irony is the fact that Cincinnati, the team we beat in the 1963 NCAA championship game, was a member of the Missouri Valley Conference at the time.

I was inducted with six others during a ceremony at the Peabody Opera House in St. Louis as part of the festivities during the MVC Men's Basketball Championship. The banquet hall was full and, right after they introduced me, they showed a short video of teammates complimenting me as a player and person. I got choked up on a number of occasion as I looked out in the audience and saw my wife and my son, Jerald, along with two of my grand-children, Kara and Kiley. That was special.

A number of Loyola staff members were on hand, as well as some of my teammates, who had made the special trip to St. Louis. I spoke mostly on team accomplishments and the trials and tribulations the team had gone through more than 50 years ago. I also got an opportunity to thank Loyola for taking a chance on me when nobody else would. I realized this was the first time I could thank my teammates and my late coach, George Ireland, who had the guts to take a major step forward and leave everybody else behind. I was also happy to see how the Missouri Valley Conference had led the way in diversity for all its sports.

I went into the MVC Hall of Fame with good company: Mick Lyon (University of Evansville), Bill Thomas (Missouri State) Anthony Parker (Bradley), Sue Daggett Miller and the late Dave Bergman (both from Illinois State). Dr. Harold Bardo (Southern Illinois) received the conference's Paul Morrison Award for Meritorious Service.

Since my wife and I are retired we were able to stay the full four days. We were treated admirably. The basketball conference competition was also excellent. The portrait of all the inductees is superb. I now have it in a special place on my wall.

I only wish my mom had been there to accept it because it all belongs to her.

Chapter 34
HEAVEN AWAITS

In late August of 2017, I got a call from Rosemarie Gold, Joe Dan's widow, who told me former Mississippi State center Bobby Shows was not doing well.

I asked for his phone number and called Bobby right away. When I reached him in the hospital I could tell he was surprised, but happy, to hear from me. I asked how he was doing. He said, "I guess okay for an old man."

I told him I had read his book, *"Level Fields of Play"* .... twice. I could tell he liked that. I also told him I felt some good things were going to happen. He asked me to keep his son, Doug posted.

I asked, "What about you?"

He said, "Jerry, I'm not doing well. But I've had some good times. As a matter of fact, that includes you and the Loyola guys.

I told him, "You know, you've been a great servant."

We wished one another well and said we would talk again soon, but it didn't happen. He died two weeks later, September 3, 2017.

In 1994, Bobby founded Sports Crusaders, "a ministry that uses sports as a tool for engaging and evangelizing young people stateside and overseas." Wherever he went to promote Sports Crusaders, Shows stood out for his 6-foot-8 frame. But I'm sure, where he is now, he stands out for his good heart, warm spirit and accomplishments.

Bobby Shows waving to the crowd.

Chapter 35
MY RELIGIOUS CONNECTIONS

I worship at Eastern Star Church "Where Jesus is Exalted and the Word is Explained" under the leadership of Jeffery A. Johnson, Sr. I have enjoyed his preaching and teaching of the Gospel of Jesus Christ over 25 years.

My friend Hoyt Diamond had been trying to get me to attend a three-day event at Second Presbyterian Church in Indianapolis for two years. Hoyt had a low-key approach but I still decided to go because anything Hoyt was involved in had to be on the up and up.

At the Great Banquet, guests from different backgrounds (spiritual and non-spiritual) come together three and half days to worship, pray, study, discussion and to break bread together. It's a chance to be still, listen, share and to hear Christ's plan for this world and our lives. It gave me a chance

Top right: Me and my Pastor of over 25 years, Jeffery A. Johnson.
Bottom photo: Great Banquet in Indianapolis

to experience God's Agape love and grace in a profound, personal way. My wife told me after attending I was a different person, both spiritually and physically. After the Great Banquet, I joined a reunion group of four or five guys that meets Saturdays for spiritual discussions and companionship. My group has been meeting for years and has been helpful in getting us through trials and tribulations of our daily lives.

Joining me at The Great Banquet are Stan, Pat and Neal.

Another outstanding spiritual program I have enjoyed is called Kairos. It's a ministry in which men go into prisons to share God's word with the prisoners. I have participated in the three-day program four times and continue to enjoy praising God through talking, singing, reading, prayer, discussion and breaking bread together.

Kairos Prison Ministry group.

It never ceases to amaze me how one bad decision or being in the wrong place at the wrong time, can make such a difference in one's life. I often wonder how my life would be different if I had not gotten off the subway and had gone through with taking money to work with the gamblers who were trying to get college players to shave points.

Many of the men in prison made a bad decision. Some of them committed horrible crimes, but they are ready and willing to turn their lives around, and through God's guidance, Kairos is there to help them.

REMINISCING

When I was in my early teens – and not playing the bongos with my Calypso Lads group – I would walk from Harlem toward downtown Manhattan. During these strolls I scoured the gutters for loose change, picking up pennies, nickels, dimes and, sometimes, quarters on my way. I would use what I collected for candy, baseball cards, movies and bus fare back to Harlem.

One afternoon around four o'clock, I started walking from 146th Street and Eighth Avenue. Before I realized it, I was at 59th Street. I had walked more than 85 blocks and collected nearly three dollars in change, including a one-dollar bill. I ended up right outside Radio City Music Hall.

Being inquisitive, I opened the door and walked into the lobby. I heard music so I opened another door and went into the theater. I saw a long line of ladies dancing, kicking up their legs in perfect alignment. I was intrigued; I had never seen such a sight. Before I knew it, a big man grabbed me by the collar and yelled "What are you doing in here?"

He roughly dragged me out to the lobby and pushed me toward the doors to the street. He cursed at me, telling me I didn't belong there and that he better not see me inside the lobby again.

I never went back to Radio City until some 40 years later. Once again, I heard the music and saw these beautiful ladies dancing in their bright red-and-white costumes. Only this time I had excellent seats, because one of the beautiful ladies dancing in unison with the Radio City Rockettes was my daughter, Julie. It was one of the proudest days of my life.

Julie Harkness Arnold

After the show, Julie waved to me to come backstage. On my way a man stopped me at the door but Julie yelled out, "Let him through, that's my Dad!"

Sometimes what goes around comes around in a better way.

Chapter 36
INDIANAPOLIS' FIRST HIGH SCHOOL CHAMPS

I've heard so many stories about the impact the Crispus Attucks High School basketball teams had on the black community in Indianapolis during 1955 and 1956, when they won consecutive state championships.

They had a theme song, called "The Crazy Song," sung to the tune of Cab Calloway's "Hi-De-Ho." Their cheerleaders performed in sync, wiggling their hips and throwing their hands in the air, then bouncing to the floor and up again to show you more. The team was the talk of the state, especially in the barber shops, hair salons and other gathering places for the black community. It was the first team from Indianapolis to win a state championship as well as the first in the country from an African American high school to do so.

I always feel a connection with the Attucks players because Loyola was the first team to have five African Americans on the floor in an NCAA Division 1 college game. I really would have cherished being a part of the community to witness the joy and excitement during that era. Black people in Harlem sometimes had something similar to experience, such as Joe Louis keeping his heavyweight title, or Jackie Robinson stealing home to lead the Dodgers to victory, or even watching the Harlem Globetrotters. To be that close to your heroes like the Attucks fans were must have been something special.

In 2015, I watched on television as Oscar Robertson and his Attucks teammates passed by on a float in the 500 Festival Parade before the Indianapolis 500. They were receiving wonderful but belated recognition for their state championships in 1955 and '56, which, many say, were reluctantly embraced by the city at the time. It reminded me of a conversation I had with Oscar years earlier as we looked out a window from the Columbia Club on the Circle downtown. He reminded me that he wouldn't have even been permitted to enter the building when he was in high school, or for years afterward.

1955-56 Crispus Attucks State Basketball Champs .

Oscar float. *Courtesty Carl Black.*

I mentioned that things had changed for black folks.

"Yeah, Jerry, they have, but we're not even close to equality yet, although we're going in the right direction," he said.

In 2017, I was back on the Circle celebrating with three predominantly black high school teams from the Indianapolis area that won state basketball championships - Ben Davis in Division 4A, Crispus Attucks in Division 3A and Tindley High School in Division 1A. Just a month earlier, I had spoken at Attucks for the History Makers Institute and was able to tell the story of the Mississippi State-Loyola game and winning the 1963 NCAA championship.

It was gratifying to be able to connect my story to recent teams, who reflected the progress that has been made since 1963. More needs to be made, but we are indeed going in the right direction.

Tinsley High School

Rob Turner who played basketball on my AAU team proudly boasted about his son R. J. Turner winning the Trester Mental Attitude Award in 4A competition at Ben Davis High.

Crispus Attucks returning to the forefront in high school basketball. This time being recognized on the circle by Congressman Andre Carson.

EPILOGUE

At least once a year, members of the 1963 championship team get together along with other standout athletes of the era to reminisce. During one of those gatherings, Jack, Rochelle and I talked about spotlighting alumni who have given back to Loyola in one way or another. The following have been recognized as of today: Frank Hogan; Dr. Paul Smulson, DDS; Art McZier; and Al and Marty Norville.

While collaborating with Loyola Athletic Director Steve Watson on putting together the event for Al and Marty, we arranged for the former players to watch the 2017-18 team scrimmage and have lunch with them afterward. About twenty former players attended, and we believed it was one of the most competitive teams we had seen in a while. Its effort and chemistry were outstanding.

Top photo: Frank Hogan, award presented by Jack Egan

Dr. Paul Smulson, DDS, award presented by Jack Egan and members of the 1963 team, along with his wife Robin Smulson.

During lunch, coach Porter Moser showed the 1963 NCAA championship game between Loyola and Cincinnati. The players really enjoyed it and began asking questions. "How did it feel winning the NCAA Championship?" "Was there a lot of hoopla?" "How did you feel being behind by fifteen points?" I was really surprised by their enthusiasm.

After the current players left, the former players talked about what we had seen. Most of us thought they would do well in the Missouri Valley Conference but weren't sure if they could win the MVC tournament; after all, Loyola hadn't been invited to the NCAA tournament in 33 years.

Jack Egan who went to a number of Loyola games, called me one evening during the season and said, "Hey, coach Porter really has these guys playing good team ball." Several of us attended the final home game of the regular season and were overjoyed when they clinched the conference championship with a 68-61 victory over Illinois State.

Caught up in the hoopla, my wife and I traveled to St. Louis for the MVC tournament at the Scottrade Center. I would be remiss if I didn't tell you how moved I was when I walked into the center and saw a poster-sized picture of me hanging with greats such as Larry Bird, Dave Stallworth, Nolan Richardson and Sidney Moncrief. The honors didn't stop there. When Loyola captured the conference tournament title over Illinois State, 65-49, behind the play of tournament MVP Donte Ingram, I was asked to present the trophy to coach Moser. It was symbolic of the 1963 team passing the trophy on to the 2018 team, and a heart-warming moment for me.

I wasn't able to attend the opening-round games of the NCAA tournament in Dallas because of a previous speaking commitment in Kentucky with Rosemarie Gold, the wife of the late Joe Dan Gold.

Symbolic of the1963 team, here I am passing on the trophy.

As we pulled up to the Fleming County Library, we heard Loyola squeak out a 64-62 win over Miami on the   radio, with Donte Ingram hitting a game-winning shot. As we
entered the library people were cheering for the underdog's success, even while Kentucky was playing. The event was great as Rosemarie and I spoke about the situations surrounding Mississippi State and Loyola in 1963.

Loyola defeated Tennessee, 63-62, in the next game. This time Clayton Custer, the MVC Player of the Year, hit the game-winning shot. The following week I was in Atlanta to see Marques Townes hit a key three-pointer to give Loyola a 69-68 win over Nevada. I never saw a team win so many close games in NCAA tournament play. Loyola finally saved our hearts with an easy 78-62 win over Kansas State in the fourth round.

Donte Ingram

After 55 years, Loyola had returned to the Final Four. I was so excited to see it happen again before I went six feet under. Sister Jean Dolores Schmidt became a national sensation as she watched the games from courtside and America fell in love with the Cinderella Ramblers.

Their success brought our 1963 Loyola team back into the spotlight. I've never been a part of such a vast amount of media coverage and was over-whelmed. I granted more than 40 telephone interviews to outlets including a Toronto radio station, WGN radio in Chicago and *Sports Illustrated* magazine.

Sister Jean and Jerry Harkness feeling good
about the team earlier in the year.

Four television stations also came out to my house in Indianapolis for interviews. Our 1963 team didn't generate nearly that much coverage when we won the championship.

It didn't end there. I received a call from a representative for TNT television who wanted me to provide color commentary on the "home team broadcast" of the semifinal game against Michigan in San Antonio. I also spoke at a gathering of basketball fans, appeared on a radio show with former Georgetown coach John Thompson and broadcaster Jim Gray and on the TBS television network with Ernie Johnson, Clark Kellogg, Kenny Smith and Charles Barkley. I had a great time with all of the appearances.

Michigan beat Loyola, 69-57, and Villanova won the tournament. But the Loyola players won hearts. I still run into people who say they were cheering for them. It was an outstanding season for a team that played with great determination and chemistry in every game. That's a winner in my book.

Ben Richardson

Loyola 2017-18 Basketball team.

CONNECTIONS

The Loyola and Mississippi State teams of 1962-63 and the Loyola team of 2017-18 had so much in common. All of the players graduated on time, had outstanding character and displayed excellent team play. Those ingredients can show what Americans can accomplish when we work together. Watching the Loyola team last season, I saw how hard coach Porter and each player worked. Their success was no fluke. As a former player, I could see how much they truly cared for each other and that was a reflection on the leadership coach Moser provided. I don't remember ever seeing so many different players hit key baskets, either. They didn't care who stepped into the spotlight, they just played the game the way it should be played. The Mississippi State team we defeated in 1963 displayed great chemistry and character as well by staring down state government officials and even some family members who didn't want them to go to the NCAA tournament to play against African Americans. Their coaches, staff worked together on a plan to overcome the social norms of the day. Sometimes the elements of success are in place and sometimes you get a little help, but it's up to you to make the connections.

Looking back at our Loyola team, I realized how hard everyone worked to get better.

Ron Miller, who was a 6-foot-2 ½ -inch center in high school, worked every day to improve his ball handling. I can see him now, dribbling behind the bleachers in the Alumni Hall gymnasium-stopping, starting, going from one side to the other, dribbling backwards, and forward, all while protecting the ball with his body. Then, after about fifteen minutes, he would shoot 10- to 15-foot jumpers over and over again from all angles. He knew he had to reinvent himself a different way in college.

Ron, like all of us practiced shooting with a smaller rim inside the basket as coach Ireland wanted us to do. Ron's shooting improved immensely. Like me, he was an average student but always presented himself well with any group of people and was poised on the court as well. He made our team so much better.

Les Hunter was not only a very talented player, he had an intimidating physique. He did us a big favor by growing two inches over the summer before he enrolled at Loyola. Had he grown earlier, he might have been recruited harder by more established programs and never come to us.

Les reached his peak in the Pros where he was nicknamed "Big Game Hunter". He was an All-Star the first two season of the league and played seven years professionally. Like most of us, Les didn't take his academics as seriously as he could have, but he was smart enough to get by. I always thought he easily could have been an A student. Les had good basketball court sense as well.

Walter Victor Rouse was an outstanding basketball player but was not heavily recruited because he was injury prone. He overcame numerous obstacles while growing up in East St. Louis. He wore braces up to his waist for the first six years of his life because of knee problems. Doctors were concerned he might never be able to walk much less play basketball. He did, but as a junior at Nashville's Pearl High School he tore the cartilage in his left knee and required surgery. The doctor advised Vic to sit out his senior year, but Vic knew if he didn't play, his basketball scholarship would be in jeopardy. I now understand the source of his incredible determination on the basketball court.

Vic also was an outstanding student who wound up earning doctorates and master degrees. He and Les Hunter had been high school teammates who won the National Negro High School championship all three of their varsity seasons. They came to Loyola in a package deal.

Jack Egan had a basketball offer from the University of Iowa out of high school. He went to campus to scrimmage with the Hawkeyes during the summer after he graduated and was happy with his performance, but the coach told him the full scholarship was no longer available to him. Perhaps if he waited until the second semester he might get another chance. Jack refused and visited the University of Houston, where a scholarship was enthusiastically offered. He asked about receiving some financial aid for law school as well, but the Houston coach could not grant that. Some of Jack's connections in Chicago then contacted coach Ireland and told him about Egan's situation.

Ireland, who had scouted Egan, (with me, ironically), was impressed with his play and agreed with Jack's request.

Loyola was Jack's third choice for college, but it worked out perfectly for all of us. Egan was a ton of fun and smart on and off the court. I'm glad he was my teammate and played with me instead of against me.

Players make most of their improvements in practice, and that's where teams are built. That's why Chuck Wood, a 6-3 junior who guarded me in practice, was so important to my development. Chuck helped me become an All-American. He sacrificed as much as anyone for our team.

Junior center Rich Rochelle, our tallest player at 6-foot-9, always played hard. Rich made us work to score around the basket. And he could score, too.

Dan Connaughton, a 6-1 sophomore guard, worked hard in practice and was arguably the best shooter on the team, especially against zone defenses.

Jim Reardon, 6-5 senior forward, was a good shooter and never complained about playing time.

Those reserves were crucial to our team's success, that's why I thought it was a great idea when John Crnokrat, a '62 grad, suggested the reserves on the 1962-63 team also go into the Loyola Sports Hall of Fame.

My connection with Loyola could not have happened by chance. I truly believe a higher power was at work.

Jackie Robinson enticed me to play high school basketball with a casual compliment while I was shooting around at the YMCA in Harlem. A dormitory burning down prevented me from going to a different college. Saying no to gamblers prevented me from going down the wrong road. coach George Ireland being hung in effigy and worried about being fired led him to take a chance on me, despite my high school grades. Speaking of grades, I never forgot how hurt and embarrassed I was not to graduate on time to march with my class. However, it gave me an extra year to play with the talented freshman team.

The most important talent I brought to the Loyola team was my physical endurance. I remember encouraging my teammates to stay up with me in the one or two mile runs and wind sprints. As a result, we were always in better shape than our opponents and that's why we were successful in our full court pressing. The regulation and overtime period by the starting five in the championship game is another example of our outstanding conditioning. I often think of my high school track coach who didn't give up on me and found my forte in distant running which continued on the Loyola basketball court.

Looking back at each one of our early experiences, it became clearer that God had a hand in selecting our team. I also believe, after becoming aware of the outstanding character of the Mississippi State players, that they were also chosen to meet the many challenges ahead in society. Every now and then God reminds us in surprising ways and at a particular time, that we must come together. It's such a good feeling when you know you have played a part in God's plan by fighting a good fight, finishing the race and keeping the faith.

A half court meeting between two captains during a trying time brought about a great friendship years later with the Gold Family.

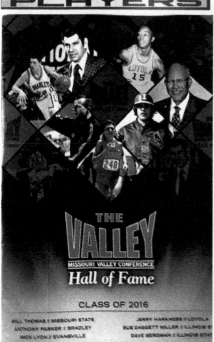

THE VALLEY

MISSOURI VALLEY CONFERENCE

Hall of Fame

CLASS OF 2016

BILL THOMAS // MISSOURI STATE   JERRY HARKNESS // LOYOLA
ANTHONY PARKER // BRADLEY   SUE DAGGETT MILLER // ILLINOIS ST
MICK LYON // EVANSVILLE   DAVE BERGMAN // ILLINOIS STATE
DR. HAROLD BARDO // SOUTHERN ILLINOIS

Books on Loyola and Mississippi State

- Ramblers .... Michael Lenehan
- Becoming Iron Men.................................. Lew Freedman
- The Ultimate Book of March Madness ... Tom Hager
- Champions for Change .... Kyle Veazey
- Level Fields of Play .... James O. Preston, Jr.